Nigel West is a military historian and journalist specializing in intelligence matters. He has researched books for a number of authors and is an acknowledged expert on his subject. He has worked on several television programmes, including the BBC's *Spy!* and *Escape!* series. His previous books include *MI5: British Security Service Operations 1909–1945*, which led to the exposure of two previously unknown spies, *A Matter of Trust: MI5: 1945–72* and *MI6: British Secret Intelligence Service Operations 1909–45*.

By the same author

Spy! (with Richard Deacon)
MI5: British Security Service Operations 1909–1945
A Matter of Trust: MI5: 1945–72
MI6: British Secret Intelligence Service Operations 1909–45

NIGEL WEST

Unreliable Witness

Espionage Myths of the Second World War

GRAFTON BOOKS
A Division of the Collins Publishing Group

LONDON GLASGOW
TORONTO SYDNEY AUCKLAND

Grafton Books
A Division of the Collins Publishing Group
8 Grafton Street, London W1X 3LA

Published by Grafton Books 1986

First published in Great Britain by
George Weidenfeld & Nicolson Limited 1984

ISBN 0-586-06629-2

Printed and bound in Great Britain by
Collins, Glasgow

Set in Times

Contents

Illustrations

The X-*Gerät* radio aerial similar to those located at Calais and Cherbourg (*photo: Fritz Trenkle*)

Mata Hari's Netherlands passport (*by courtesy of Sam Wagenaar*)

The French identity card forged by M16 for Halina Szymanska (*M. Fabian*)

HMS *Royal Oak* (*Imperial War Museum*)

The victorious U-47 returns to Kiel, 23 October 1939 (© *Ferdinand Urbahns*)

Bernd Ruland, a warrant officer in the communications centre of the Wehrmacht High Command (*by courtesy of Schweizer Verlagshaus*)

Three teleprinter operators at the German High Command's secret communications centre (*by courtesy of Schweizer Verlagshaus*)

A *geheimschreiber* operator preparing a message for automatic transmission along teleprinter lines (*by courtesy of Schweizer Verlagshaus*)

Alexander Foote, the British-born wireless operator who ran one of the LUCY ring's three illegal Soviet radios in Switzerland (© *Police Cantonale, Lausanne*)

Alexander Rado, the Hungarian leader of the LUCY ring (© *Ringier Bilderdienst*)

Rudolf Roessler, the LUCY ring's key figure (*by courtesy of Pierre Accoce*)

Dusko Popov, the Yugoslav double agent (*photo: Robert Markel, 1973*)

Commander Philip Johns, the British SIS Head of Station in Lisbon (*by courtesy of Philip Johns*)

Acknowledgements

I am indebted to the following people who have been kind enough to help my research: the staff of the British Museum and the Public Record Office at Kew; Sir William Stephenson, who has granted me three interviews at his home in Bermuda; H. Montgomery Hyde and Bill Ross-Smith, both members of Sir William Stephenson's wartime staff at British Security Co-ordination in New York; Professor John Campbell of McMaster University, who has undertaken a study of Operation JUBILEE; BALLOON, DREADNOUGHT, GARBO, GELATINE, TATE, BRUTUS, MUTT and JEFF, all former MI5 double agents; the late Dusko Popov, code-named TRICYCLE; Jean Overton Fuller, MADELEINE's biographer and friend; Madame Halina Szymanska, who acted as an intermediary for Admiral Canaris in Switzerland; Frederick Rubin, whose fluency in Russian and Hungarian has proved invaluable; Bob Hambly of the Camp X Military Museum at Oshawa, Ontario; Anne Fleming, Deputy Keeper of the Imperial War Museum's Department of Film; David Tinch, Chief Librarian at Kirkwall, Orkney; the staff of the Nationality Division of the Home Office who kindly checked their pre-war naturalization files; Philip Knightley, who now owns a photograph of a pre-war photograph of an Anglo-German Fellowship dinner; Professor M. R. D. Foot, who recalled the circumstances in which he drew up a map of the SOE networks in France; and Jean Howard, for her guidance over MOONLIGHT SONATA and her generosity with her collection of *Die Nachhut*.

Finally, I owe a debt of thanks to my researcher, Camilla van Gerbig, and the numerous retired MI5 and SIS officers who have patiently guided me but cannot be named.

Introduction

It is high time that this spy business was debunked. Several hundred books on secret service have appeared since the war; of these, about one per cent have been strictly accurate, a larger proportion founded on fact, but the greater part have been the sheerest of fiction – while pretending to be true!

BERNARD NEWMAN in *Spy*

The amount of misinformation that has appeared in print and then been elevated to history through constant repetition is appalling.

DAVID C. MARTIN in *Wilderness of Mirrors*

The secret world of intelligence is surrounded by mystique. The very nature of espionage makes it a difficult subject to research and it is often well-nigh impossible to establish exactly what took place during a particular event. In wartime, intelligence operations are shrouded necessarily with a further layer of secrecy, which conspires to confuse and deceive. Whenever books come to be written about celebrated (or notorious) incidents, errors creep in and history becomes distorted. Confronted by an official reluctance to set the record straight, authors tend to rely on each other's material and in so doing compound previous errors.

Occasionally these slips take on an importance of their own, especially when they are linked to events of significance. Dozens, perhaps hundreds of people may have contributed to the success of an operation but, as like as not, each will recollect a different aspect of it. In the absence of official comment one highly coloured opinion may be repeated and exaggerated, thereby trans-forming the original story. But whose views are right? What really did take place?

The Great War of 1914–18 had its share of what might be termed 'intelligence myths'. Mata Hari, who could easily lay claim to the title of most famous spy of the century, has had six books, three films and a musical created around her. Most have perpetuated her own claims to have been a Hindu temple dancer from an exotic Eurasian background. In fact, Marguerite MacLeod was nothing of the kind. She was a bored, disappointed, Dutch army wife who fantasized a bogus past for herself. According to some contemporary reports, she was not even physically attractive. In any event her birth certifi-cate, dated 7 August 1876, makes her over forty when she was executed in Paris in 1917.

Similarly, many people consider Nurse Cavell to have been a British spy. The distinguished historian Professor M. R. D. Foot has referred to 'Nurse Cavell's secret parallel career as an intelligence agent'.[1] Certainly she was executed by the Germans in October 1915 'for treason in time of war in having led recruits to the enemy', but she was never charged with espionage. Indeed, even a former Secret Intelligence Service officer, Henry Landau, has argued what was, essentially, the German case. At the end of the Great War he was instructed to investigate the background to Miss Cavell's arrest and execution. He concluded that, although the nurse's escape organization had helped many Allied soldiers reach their own lines, she had never herself been a spy: 'I know definitely that Miss Cavell and the leading members of her organization were not engaged in espionage . . .'[2]

The purpose of this book is to examine some of the more enduring intelligence myths of the last war and trace their provenance. Did Churchill really receive advance warning from Bletchley of the Luftwaffe's attack on Coventry? Did President Roosevelt deliberately suppress important information concerning the Japanese attack on Pearl Harbor? Was the RAF enticed into an aerial trap over Nuremberg?

In the post-war years many books have been written on these controversial subjects. Some have been flatly contradicted by others. Who is right? Which author has proved the most reliable? Why should the opinion of one observer be considered better than another? Should the comments of an actual participant rate higher than the view taken by an historian sifting through the records several decades later?

Wartime intelligence operations are always cloaked in secrecy, and sometimes the relevant files are never released to the public. But in recent years a growing volume of secret documents has been declassified and found its way into the public domain. In 1977, for example, the first ULTRA decrypts were released to the Public Record Office, causing historians to revise many of their past judgements.

The veil of secrecy was lifted further by the publication in 1979 of the first volume of an official history of *British Intelligence in the Second World War*. Professor Hinsley's team of researchers were granted unprecedented access to the Registries of various secret organizations and, as a result, light has been shed on a traditionally murky area of history. Perhaps encouraged by this relaxation of convention, a number of retired intelligence officers have broken their silence and have assisted those delving into these hitherto prohibited topics.

By analysing the impressively authoritative material contained in the current three volumes of the official history, and by persuading certain individuals to 'break cover', new insight can be gained into particular intelligence operations. Some, such as the ill-fated raid on Dieppe, have previously been matters of speculation combined with guesswork and hindsight.

Some of the stories that follow concern the activities of those most complex of spies, the double agents. It has been alleged that Allied double agents played crucial roles in Operation MARKET GARDEN at Arnhem, in the success of the famous LUCY ring in Switzerland, and in the identification of the Nazi spy known as CICERO. But, like the agents themselves, nothing is quite what it seems. Double agents and their respective case officers weave deliberately tangled webs of deception around themselves, and even the business of translating their code-names into real names can prove dishearteningly complicated.

Take, as an illustration, the true identities of two of MI5's famed wartime double agents, code-named MUTT and JEFF. These two men had been recruited as German spies in Norway and sent on a mission to Scotland in March 1941. Soon after their arrival in Banffshire they had been taken into custody and both had become enthusiastic double agents, sending misleading messages to their Abwehr controllers until February 1944. What were their real names, and what had become of them after the war? One author claimed to know the inside story. In 1971 the American historian Ladislas Farago said that he had accidentally stumbled on 800 yellow boxes of microfilm containing the Abwehr's complete secret archives. When I visited Farago in New York, he told me that the sealed boxes had lain undisturbed in the American National Archives since the war and were full of extraordinary secrets, including the records that revealed the identities of MUTT and JEFF. In *Game of the Foxes* Farago says of them: 'They went by a string of pseudonyms and registry numbers, but today we know that their real names were Olaf Klausen and Jack Berg.'[3]

I tried to track down Klausen and Berg, but instead of finding them I unearthed a book written in 1958 which had been based on the 'secret service war diaries of General Erwin Lahousen'. Lahousen was credited by the two authors, Charles Wighton and Gunter Peis, as having been the head of the Abwehr's sabotage division. Both MUTT and JEFF had been named: 'They were Jack Berg, a hairdresser in his middle twenties, and his friend Olav Klausen, about the same age and formerly a sergeant in the Norwegian Army.'[4]

Lahousen's evidence seemed to confirm Farago's discovery in the Abwehr's secret archives. Or did it? The next book I found which mentioned two Norwegian agents was *The Secrets of D-Day*, which won the 1964 Prix de la Resistance and was written by Jacques Peyroles under the pseudonym 'Gilles Perrault'. He claimed that, according to an Abwehr report,

the Luftwaffe had bombed two towns in Scotland as a diversion when money and explosives were being dropped on 20 February 1943. The civilian casualties had been heavy. And the two Norwegians had been previously informed of the raid to be made on the towns near the dropping area. Would the British have deliberately sacrificed the lives of thousands of women and children in order to make the enemy believe that the two agents were still operating freely?[5]

I discovered that Fraserburgh had been bombed that night but the sole casualty had been one child. Had this anything to do with MUTT and JEFF?

With more than a little unofficial help from intelligence sources, I was able to trace JEFF to Norway, where he was living under his real name, Tor Glad. We met in Oslo and he kindly put me in touch with his former partner, John Moe, alias MUTT, who was then living near Malmö in Sweden. Neither man had heard of Farago's book, and were somewhat bemused to learn of 'Klausen' and 'Berg'. Both recounted their experiences to me and I learnt how Fraserburgh had come to be bombed. A wartime plan, Operation OATMEAL, had been mounted to persuade MUTT and JEFF's German controllers to supply them with extra equipment by air. The plan called for a single Luftwaffe plane to parachute a canister containing money and a wireless transmitter into a dropping zone on the east coast of Scotland.

Initially the operation had gone well, and the canister had been retrieved by MUTT and his MI5 escort. Unfortunately, and unexpectedly, the German pilot then decided to round off the evening by dropping a stick of bombs on the nearby fishing port of Fraserburgh. An eleven-year-old boy was killed in the raid and John Moe had been deeply upset. He had later transmitted a complaint to the Germans, claiming that the Luftwaffe's action had caused chaos and the extra police activity had endangered his mission by preventing him from leaving the area. As a result, he added, he had been obliged to spend two uncomfortable nights out in the open. The Abwehr apologized and undertook to prevent the Luftwaffe from repeating the exercise. The next time OATMEAL was staged, it was not accompanied by an air raid. Moe also wrote to the Mayor of Fraserburgh expressing his condolences.

During the course of the Second World War there were many other occasions when an espionage myth was allowed to take root, flourish, and then bloom in works of serious history. A case in point is that of Dorothy O'Grady.

Dorothy O'Grady now lives in Sandown, a seaside town in the Isle of Wight, but in August 1940 she was arrested on a charge of espionage after she had been found acting suspiciously near an army camp. She confessed to being a German spy and was tried at Winchester Assizes. It was only after she had pleaded guilty and had been sentenced to death by Mr Justice McNaughten that she had admitted that her confession had been an invention. She had never spied for anyone. Her Counsel, John Trapnell KC, had arranged an Appeal and, with the agreement of the Crown, her conviction on the capital charge had been quashed. Instead, she had received fourteen years' imprisonment for breaking the Defence Regulations. Although the exact details of the case were not made public at the time, the press did report both the trial and the Appeal. Nevertheless, Mrs O'Grady became known as a notorious spy. When, in 1950, the *Daily Telegraph*'s crime correspondent, Stanley Firmin, gave an account of her case in *They Came to Spy*, he insisted that Mrs O'Grady 'had been arrested when it was found she was cutting vital military telephone wires'[6] and concluded: 'But she was a spy for Germany. There was not the slightest doubt about that.'[7]

By confirming that O'Grady was a genuine spy, as opposed to the deluded, lonely woman she really was, Firmin had helped create a myth. It was later taken up by a military historian, Jock Haswell, who included Firmin's erroneous version of Mrs O'Grady's tale in his study of *The Intelligence and Deception of the D-Day Landings*, and even embroidered it a little. Mrs O'Grady, he claimed,

kept a boarding house in the Isle of Wight and sent information, written in the crudest of invisible inks, to a handler in Portugal. Motivated by greed and hatred, and entirely untrained, she was not in a position to provide anything of much value.[8]

Clearly Haswell had succumbed to the O'Grady myth and had ensured its longevity. But at least Mrs O'Grady had really existed. The most elusive of secret agents are those that simply never had. While reviewing the miserable effort made by the Germans to spy in England during the war Haswell revealed the existence of Hans Sorensen:

> In the motley crowd of men and women who floated down or came ashore to discover where or when the Allies would attack Hitler's Fortress Europe, there was only one man, Hans Sorensen, who was known to be a spy and interrogated at great length but made no mistake.[9]

Where had Sorensen appeared from? None of MI5's wartime staff had ever heard of him, although an author named Bernard Newman had already recounted his exploits. Newman was the author of eighty-eight books, of which many were on the subject of espionage and published by The Right Book Club. As well as being a prolific author of non-fiction, he also wrote more than a dozen detective thrillers under the pen-name Don Betteridge. In *Spies in Britain* Newman had claimed to have met Sorensen in Hamburg after the war. He said: 'I already knew quite a lot about Herr "Sorensen", but when he had filled up the gaps in my knowledge his spy story was revealed as one of the most fantastic of the war.'[10]

According to Newman, Hans Sorensen had been one of a group of five German agents sent to engage in sabotage operations in England sometime in the spring of 1941. Although 'he did not speak English' Sorensen and his companions had apparently arrived in Helmsdale, on the north-east coast of Scotland, and had posed as deserters from the German army of occupation in Norway. Their mission had been to join the Pioneer

Corps as anti-Nazis, but Newman maintained that after seven months of interrogation 'involving the cream of the British Intelligence Service', all five were interned.

Some aspects of the story were difficult to check because Newman confirmed that 'Sorensen' had not been the agent's real name. Those details that could be checked proved to be entirely fictitious. Certainly no group of German deserters had sailed into Helmsdale in the spring of 1941 (or at any other time during the war). Nevertheless, Newman's imaginary spy had surfaced again, fifteen years later, in Jock Haswell's book and had become established.

Together Firmin and Newman were responsible for the propagation of dozens more myths in the realm of espionage and intelligence. One of Newman's more bizarre inventions is the story in *Spy Catchers* of the German spy named Karl Werfel. Allegedly, Werfel had 'escaped' to England posing as a Belgian refugee, but had eventually been arrested and executed at Wandsworth. According to Newman, Werfel had been trained as a spy at a special German school. There he had 'studied practical espionage under a tutor named Vogel'.[11] Newman revealed that Vogel had, in reality, been working for the British and had betrayed the identities of all his pupils.

Among the meticulously kept records of British wartime executions there is no mention of any Karl Werfel. Nor is there a case even remotely similar to Werfel's. Only three Germans had been executed at Wandsworth and none bore any resemblance to Werfel. Could the improbable tale of Herr Vogel be true anyway? Evidently Jock Haswell thought so: 'When war was declared on 3 September 1939 the police had a list of practically all the agents in the second network, because the Abwehr instructor was a member of MI6.'[12]

The invention of Karl Werfel and the misrepresentation

of Dorothy O'Grady are but two relatively trivial incidents which demonstrate how overenthusiasm, poor research or a combination of both can end in fiction acquiring a mantle of fact. The cases that will be examined in the pages that follow have rather more significance, not least to the intelligence officers who participated in them and who, generously, have enabled the truth to be disentangled from fantasy.

1

Moonlight Sonata or Sacrifice?

At about 5.30 on 14 November, Group Captain Addison of 80
Wing rang Jones to tell him that his listening aircraft had been
up and that the 'Rivers' beams seemed to be set for a town in
the Midlands: Could Jones let him know the Germans' target?
As Jones stated in the 1977 BBC television programme *The
Secret War*: 'I did not know. The Enigma had not [been] broken
that night in time, although it had by the following morning . . .
but that was too late. So I couldn't tell him where the target
was.'

BRIAN JOHNSON in *The Secret War*[1]

On the night of 14 November 1940 449 German bombers
flew across Britain to the heart of the industrial Midlands
and devastated the city of Coventry. The civilian losses
were unprecedented, and more than 550 people were
killed. A further 1,000 were seriously injured. Then in
1974, Group Captain F. W. Winterbotham, in his book
The Ultra Secret, suggested that the air raid thirty-four
years earlier had been known about in advance. Could
action have been taken to save lives? Fred Winterbotham,
relying on his memory, suggested that a mistake had
been made by a German cipher clerk on the afternoon of
the raid which led the Bletchley decrypters to discover
the target scheduled for that night's attack. Churchill
had been informed immediately that Coventry had been
singled out by the Luftwaffe, but the Prime Minister had
decided against the general evacuation of the inhabitants
in order to preserve ULTRA's security. Winterbotham
explained that Goering had decided to bomb other cities
besides London, but the names of those chosen were

in code. 'However, at about 3 P.M. on November the fourteenth someone must have made a slip up and instead of a city with a code-name, Coventry was spelt out.'[2]

Winterbotham, who had acted as an information link between the Secret Intelligence Service's headquarters at Broadway and the decrypters at Bletchley Park in Buckinghamshire, recalled telephoning Downing Street with the news: 'Churchill was at a meeting so I spoke to his personal secretary and told him what had happened.'

Winterbotham, therefore, suggests that Churchill was confronted with a stark choice: to order the evacuation of Coventry, thus jeopardizing the future of his 'most secret source', or simply to send a discreet warning to the city's emergency services. Winterbotham adds that:

This is the sort of terrible decision that sometimes has to be made on the highest levels in war. It was unquestionably the right one, but I am glad it was not I who had to make it. Official history maintains that the Air Ministry had two days' notice of this raid. As far as Ultra was concerned it was now definite.[3]

Thus it appears that in one of those all-too-frequent agonizing decisions which invariably fall to war leaders, Churchill got his priorities right and protected ULTRA, at the expense of a few thousand avoidable civilian casualties in a city populated by a quarter of a million people.

Eighteen months after Winterbotham had made his controversial disclosures another author, Anthony Cave Brown, elaborated on them in his massive account of wartime deception, *Bodyguard of Lies*. He was equally emphatic that Churchill had been given advance warning of the raid, although he differed from Winterbotham on the issue of when exactly Coventry had been positively identified as the target. According to his account: 'Ultra

gave Churchill and his advisers at least forty-eight, possibly sixty, hours' warning of the devastating raid that
was planned for Coventry.'[4] Cave Brown also described
Churchill's unenviable dilemma:

> But if no extraordinary defensive measure could be taken to
> protect Coventry, might not a confidential warning that their
> city was about to be attacked on a large scale be given to civic
> authorities and to the fire-fighting, ambulance and hospital
> services? Should not the population of the inner city, together
> with the aged, the young, and those in hospitals who could be
> moved, be evacuated? To all these propositions, Churchill said
> no; there must be no evacuations and no warnings.[5]

Finally, Cave Brown concurs with Winterbotham that
the Prime Minister's decision to save ULTRA was the
correct one to make: 'It was a tragic decision for Churchill
to have to make, but it was the only way to protect
Ultra.'[6]

In his book *A Man Called Intrepid*, published in 1976,
William Stevenson took the same line as Winterbotham
and Cave Brown, and shed new light on the mistake
made by the German cipher clerk previously referred to:
'In the second week of November in 1940, Bletchley
obtained the German order to destroy Coventry. The
name came through in plain text.'[7]

With such imprecise dating it is impossible to determine
the exact day that Stevenson believes the Prime Minister
was advised that Coventry had been selected, but on one
point Stevenson is absolutely certain: 'The name of the
target was in Churchill's hands within minutes of Hitler's
decision.'[8]

Whatever the timing of this remarkable achievement,
the effect on Churchill had been much the same. He had
been faced with a limited set of alternatives: 'If the Prime
Minister evacuated Coventry, as he so desperately wished

to do, he would tell the enemy that he knew their plans . . . If the citizens were not warned, thousands would die or suffer.'[9]

Did Churchill really have to make such a heart-rending decision? Air Ministry papers recently released to the public now prove that the Prime Minister was never presented with such a choice. What really happened is quite different, and rather more complex.

In October and November 1940 the RAF was receiving information concerning the Luftwaffe's future plans from no less than four different sources. The Directorate of Air Intelligence at the Air Ministry had responsibility for co-ordinating all four, and took an active role in two in particular: the interrogation of prisoners of war and the examination of captured enemy documents. Captured aircrews were routinely separated and deposited at a special prisoner-of-war cage at Trent Park, Cockfosters, where they were questioned by skilled interrogators attached to the I(k) section of Air Intelligence. Reports from AI I(k) were delivered on a daily basis to the Director of Air Intelligence, Charles Medhurst, at the Air Ministry in London and then compared to information received from other sources. Another AI section, I(f), consisted of air-crash examiners who would visit the scene of every downed enemy plane (preferably before the souvenir hunters had got hold of it) and search the wreckage for maps, instruction manuals and unusual equipment. Any interesting finds were transported to specialist sub-sections for detailed analysis. Once again, these AI units submitted regular reports to the Air Ministry. An illuminating account of their work has been given by S. John Peskett in *Strange Intelligence*.

AI's other two useful sources were of a rather more technical nature. During the summer of 1940 the RAF's main signals interception station at Cheadle had detected the introduction of a German navigational aid, apparently designed to guide Luftwaffe bombers on to their targets. [10] The system, known as *Knickebein* (literally, 'crooked leg'), was of considerable assistance to the Luftwaffe crews at night because, at that stage of the war, they were relatively inexperienced at navigating in the dark. A *Knickebein* transmitter in Europe sent a continuous dot-dash signal along a narrow beam, creating a radio path for the aircraft to follow. A second beacon sent another signal which bisected the first at the exact point at which the bombers were to drop their cargo. Later in the summer two improved systems, known as X-*Gerät* and Y-*Gerät*, were introduced to give the Luftwaffe greater accuracy. All three aids held considerable promise for the RAF, who set to work to develop counter-measures as soon as the operating frequencies had been established. If the navigational paths could be monitored, the Luftwaffe's targets might be discovered; if the beams could be deflected without discovery there was every chance that future raids might be diverted to areas where they could do little or no damage. [11]

In addition to these sources there was information coming in from the code-breakers at Bletchley devoted to the decryption and analysis of Luftwaffe operational orders. Their task was made a little easier by the fact that German Luftwaffe machine ciphers (encoded on the now famous Enigma machine) were the very first to be broken on a regular basis. Furthermore, as well as using the Enigma to transmit messages concerning routine operational matters, the Luftwaffe also used the same system to advise individual units of details concerning their *Knickebein* signals. Each air wing received the frequencies and approximate headings of the beams, and the times of the transmission tests which usually took place three or four hours before take-off to enable every aircraft to

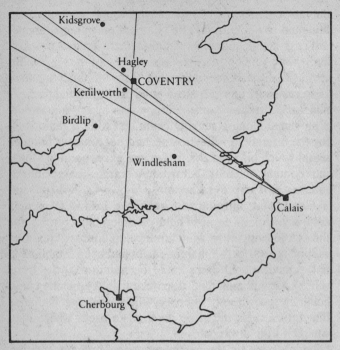

The German navigation beams and the RAF's jammers. At 1300 on 14 November 1940 the RAF intercepted the first calibration signals of the enemy's X-*Gerät* directional beams. By 1500 it had discovered that the beams were intersecting over Coventry. The primary beam gave the Luftwaffe bomb aimer advance notice of the target's approach. A second beam, fifteen kilometres from the target, gave an audible signal inside the aircraft, and the final beam indicated the exact spot for the release of the bombs. The RAF was confident that its electronic counter-measures, code-named COLD WATER, would interfere with the beams but its five jammers were set to the wrong frequency and had no effect. Contrary to many published accounts, ULTRA played no part in the identification of Coventry as the German target on the day of the raid.

check its equipment. By intercepting these signals Bletchley was sometimes able to predict forthcoming night attacks; identifying possible targets was to come much later.

An Air Intelligence summary dated 18 October 1940 correctly forecast an increase in Luftwaffe night attacks and acknowledged that future air raids might focus around a new strategy of concentrated blitzes using several hundred bombers at a time. On 11 November came advance warning of the first such mass attack, apparently codenamed MOONLIGHT SONATA. Although no individual targets were specified (beyond a list of four target numbers), Air Intelligence did deduce some information from the code-name itself. They advised that the first half indicated an operation timed to take advantage of the full moon (the next, it was noted, was due on 15 November), and that the second half suggested a three-phase sequence. By the time the Bletchley decrypters had completed their work the signal was already two days old. Nevertheless, another significant piece of intelligence was extracted from the Enigma text itself: a *Knickebein* beacon was to be used, which implied a night attack, and the captured documents section noted that they had recently acquired a Luftwaffe map with four definite target areas drawn on it. All four were in south-east England. When all this information was combined a pattern emerged. The Luftwaffe was planning a mass raid, guided by radio beams, on or soon after the full moon of 15 November. The only note of dissent came from a report submitted by AI I(k) which had arrived on 12 November. In it the interrogators at Cockfosters summarized a conversation overheard between a bomber pilot, who had been captured on 9 November, and a British *agent provocateur* or 'stool-pigeon'. Earlier in the war the Security Service, MI5, had recruited several

German-speaking refugees for work in the internment camps. Most were anti-Nazis from Austria and they volunteered to masquerade as fellow prisoners of war and extract information from recently captured prisoners. Similar schemes during the Great War had yielded excellent intelligence at very little risk. As it turned out, a high proportion of prisoners of war were prepared to confide in complete strangers in their first vulnerable hours in captivity. Thereafter they tended to regain their self-control and were less inclined to be indiscreet.

According to AI I(k), the recently captured bomber pilot had mentioned a massive Luftwaffe raid scheduled for the period 15–20 November and destined for Coventry and Birmingham. This was the first occasion that Coventry had been mentioned anywhere by name, and the intelligence had not come from a decrypt. The memo from Trent Park, Cockfosters, now available in the Public Record Office,[12] also contains two qualifications: 'I thought it well to bring this information to your notice although on account of the source it should be treated with reserve as he is untried.' The memo concluded:

I believe that Squadron Leader Humphreys [from Bletchley] has pretty definite information that the attack is to be against London and the Home Counties and he believes that it is in retaliation for Munich. The objective should be regarded as doubtful as probably his information is later.

In the face of this caution, and the suggestion that Humphreys' news was more recent, Air Intelligence headquarters began to plan on the assumption that London, and towns in the area for forty miles around London, were the most likely targets for a massed attack and, on the morning of 14 November, informed the Prime Minister that the targets, 'which are probably alternative to each other, are Central London (not absolutely definite),

Greater London, the area bounded by Farnborough-Maidenhead-Reading and the area bounded by Rochester-Favisham-Isle of Sheppey'. In a further paragraph Churchill was told by the Air Staff: 'We believe that the target areas will be those noted in paragraph 1 above, probably in the vicinity of London, but if further information indicates Coventry, Birmingham or elsewhere, we hope to get instructions out in time.'

The memo is optimistic about the chances of taking precautions, because the original Enigma decrypt had mentioned the Germans' intention to transmit a test signal from the relevant navigation beacon at 1300 hours on the afternoon of the raid. This would identify the final choice of target. Once the RAF had traced these signals, they also hoped to be able to jam them. A special plan of counter-measures, code-named COLD WATER, was ready to be deployed.

Soon after 1300 hours on 14 November the RAF's interception unit at Kingsdown reported that the Germans had begun test transmissions. This was at least twenty-four hours earlier than Air Intelligence had led everyone to believe: full moon being on 15 November. Two hours later Kingsdown had calculated the route of the beam: the target was confirmed as Coventry and not any of the three areas around London. This news must have been somewhat disconcerting, but in terms of the counter-measures the location of the target was largely irrelevant. COLD WATER depended only on knowing the frequency of the German signals, and this vital information had been communicated to the RAF's jammers by 1500 hours, in plenty of time to activate COLD WATER. Unfortunately, COLD WATER failed to work. No. 80 Wing RAF were given the wrong frequency and their jammers had no impact on the German beams.[13] The unit entrusted with the radio counter-measures was centred on the Mildmay Institute at Garston, near Watford. COLD WATER also called for a British counter-attack on twenty-seven Luftwaffe airfields on the Continent and the destruction of the X-*Gerät* transmitter in Cherbourg. Both initiatives were executed by the RAF (with the loss of ten bombers), but No. 80 Wing's failure to set their jammers on the correct frequency ensured that the enemy found their target and delivered their bombs.

In retrospect it is easy to see how the various authors, ignorant of the work of Air Intelligence or the full background of COLD WATER, should have concluded from Winterbotham's remarks that the Prime Minister had made a deliberate decision to protect ULTRA's future at the expense of a city in the Midlands. In the event Churchill presumed he had no need to order the evacuation of Coventry as he had good reason to believe that adequate counter-measures were available: so far as he knew, the German bombs would fall, but on empty fields.

The crucial difference between the accounts of Cave Brown and Stevenson on the one hand, and Winterbotham on the other, lies in the actual timing of the positive identification of MOONLIGHT SONATA's target. Winterbotham recalls how he passed on news at about 3 P.M. (1500 hours) on the day itself, but this news did not come from ULTRA. It was Kingsdown's calculations on the route of the beam confirming Coventry which were sent via Air Intelligence. Winterbotham must have forgotten the source of the material he passed on and evidently he was unaware of COLD WATER, which, as we have seen, was deployed and failed. Stevenson's version, describing the options available to Churchill, over-accentuates the problem. It is equally clear that the name Coventry never appeared in any ULTRA decrypts. As the official history of *British Intelligence in the Second*

World War acknowledges on page 534, no decrypts on 14 November 1940 alerted either Bletchley, Air Intelligence or Downing Street to the possibility of an imminent raid or the name of Coventry itself. Those details came from other sources.

2

Canaris: Traitor or Hero?

Canaris' whole career was one which did not suggest he was any better than a good German patriot and in some respects he was a downright scoundrel . . .

RICHARD DEACON in *A History of the British Secret Service*

Canaris impressed me not as a man of action but as an observer and a philosopher, perhaps the most reflective member of the German military that I had met.

HANS VON HERWARTH in *Against Two Evils*

His parallel is not in history but in literature. He was the Hamlet of conservative Germany.

HUGH TREVOR-ROPER in *The Philby Affair: Espionage, Treason and Secret Services*

There have often been suggestions that Admiral Wilhelm Canaris, who later became head of the German Abwehr, met Mata Hari during the First World War. It has also been suggested by others that he met Stewart Menzies, later to become Chief of the British Secret Intelligence Service during the Second World War. Further stories suggest that Canaris supplied useful information to his British counterpart in 1941. I would now like to examine these three Canaris episodes in detail.

To date three English-language biographies have been published about Canaris, but very little has been written about Menzies. The reason is understandable. Canaris was executed in Flossenburg concentration camp in April 1945 for complicity in the 20 July plot against Hitler, and thus became something of a legend. Menzies, on the other hand, continued to head the Secret Intelligence Service until his retirement in 1952. By convention his name was rarely used in public while he remained in office, and few people were aware of his identity until it became quite widely publicized on the publication of *The Quiet Canadian* by H. Montgomery Hyde in 1962.

Canaris had enjoyed an extraordinary career. As a junior naval officer aboard the German cruiser *Dresden* he had seen action in the Battle of the Falklands. In April 1915 the *Dresden* was scuttled in Chilean waters and the crew interned. Undeterred, Canaris escaped and, armed with forged identity papers, trekked across the Andes to Buenos Aires, where he boarded a steamer bound for neutral Holland via Falmouth. The port authorities at Falmouth were fooled by ·Canaris's faked travel documents and he continued his journey to Berlin, where he reported for duty in October 1915. Instead of posting him to a new ship, the German Admiralty gave him a secret mission in Madrid. Details of his work in Spain are sketchy, in spite of the post-war discovery of his service records (now in the Institute of Contemporary History in Munich), and, as a result, there has been considerable speculation about his alleged connections with secret agents, including the famous Mata Hari.

The basis of this particular myth seems to rest on the idea that Canaris and Mata Hari, whose real name, although she was Dutch, was Mrs Marguerite MacLeod, were both living in the Spanish capital at the same time, and that the ill-fated Dutch woman was in touch with the naval attaché at the German Embassy in Madrid. According to Kurt Singer, in *Spies and Traitors of World War II*, the relationship 'developed into a passionate love affair'.[1]

Once recruited by the German secret service as a spy with the code-number H-21, Mrs MacLeod is supposed

to have travelled to Paris and begun work in earnest for
Canaris. Then, on some unknown date in 1917, Mata
Hari apparently returned to Spain for a final meeting
with her lover. Singer suggests that he was disgruntled at
seeing her, but 'they finally made up and spent a week
together'.[2]

Reassured, Mata Hari returned to her illicit activities
in France and was arrested for espionage and executed.
The crux of the prosecution's case was that she had come
to Paris under the cover of Holland's neutrality to obtain
French military secrets. Since it is known that Mrs
MacLeod was arrested by the French on 12 February
1917 and shot at Vincennes after being found guilty of
spying for the Germans on 15 October, her reunion with
Canaris presumably must have taken place within the
first six weeks of 1917. This sequence of events is flawed
because Canaris was transferred to U-boats in October
1916. During the first two months of 1917 Canaris was
attending a training course at the submarine school at
Eckernförde. If this second tryst was merely a figment of
Singer's imagination, what of the first? A comparison of
the known movements of Mrs MacLeod and Canaris is
illuminating.

According to the official stamps on her Dutch passport,
which was retained by the French Ministry of War after
her execution, the first time she visited Spain was in June
1916 while travelling from The Hague to Paris. Wartime
conditions made such a lengthy route necessary; she had
left Holland on the Royal Dutch Lloyd liner SS *Zeelandia*
on 24 May 1916, and reached the Spanish capital on 12
June. Two days later she resumed her journey by train
and crossed the French frontier at Hendaye. She arrived
in Paris on 16 June.

Mata Hari next entered Spain by train at Irun early in
November 1916, apparently trying to return to The

Hague. After a brief stop at Madrid she continued her roundabout journey from Paris to Holland. She caught the SS *Hollandia* at Vigo, but was detained and questioned by British police officers at Falmouth. She was released but, instead of going on to Amsterdam, she returned to Madrid, where she took up residence in the Palace Hotel. She remained there from 10 December 1916 to 2 January 1917. Thus the legendary spy made two brief trips to Madrid, and one longer visit. Canaris's service record shows that he left Berlin on 30 November 1915 and arrived in Madrid a few days later, having travelled overland through Italy and France on his forged Chilean identity papers.

Contrary to Singer's claim that 'Canaris was ostensibly a military attaché to Spain', the naval officer had only minimal contact with Embassy personnel and was never diplomatically accredited. His personal file shows that he left Spain on 21 February 1916, posing as a Chilean *en route* to a tuberculosis clinic in Switzerland. He was arrested in Genoa by the Italian police, but somehow managed to escape back to Spain, where he reappeared on 15 March. Meanwhile the German Naval staff were expressing some anxiety about Canaris and a number of telegrams survive demanding that he report for duty at the Baltic Command's U-boat headquarters. Finally, on 30 September 1916, Canaris was able to rendezvous with U-35 off Cartagena. Nine days later Canaris was delivered safely to Germany.

From the events described above it is clear that, apart from a three-week interlude in Italy over February/March 1916, Canaris spent the period December 1915 to September 1916 in Spain, and was therefore unavailable to develop a liaison with Mata Hari on two of the three occasions she visited Madrid. For the Canaris-Mata Hari relationship to have been true, it needs to have taken

place during her first brief forty-eight-hour stop-over in
Madrid in mid-June 1916: the only time they overlapped.
Could it have happened?

That question can only be answered by looking at the
activities of the German intelligence officers based in
Madrid during this period. The issue has been complicated by the differing accounts given about who exactly
recruited Mata Hari as a German agent. In 1930 her first
biographer, Major Thomas Coulson, referred to a series
of newspaper stories in the Madrid newspaper *El Liberal*
which, allegedly,

spoke quite frankly of the relations between the chief of the
German espionage service in Madrid and the dancer who was
staying at the Ritz Hotel. The Allied officers in the capital were
already aware that Mata Hari had been employed by von Kroon
before these articles were published, but this showed that
the dancer was burning her boats publicly in having herself
proclaimed as a German spy.[3]

So Lieutenant von Kroon 'took Mata Hari into his employ
as well as into the intimacy of his friendship'. Yet the
transcript of Mata Hari's interrogation by the French
authorities names a certain Major von Kalle as the first
and only German officer she had communicated with in
Madrid – in December 1916. It seems likely that Coulson's
'von Kroon' was an erroneous reference to the German
naval attaché in Madrid, Lieutenant-Commander Hans
von Krohn.

'Von Kalle' was unquestionably the German military
attaché in Madrid, Major Kalle. Supporting evidence for
this can be found in documents used at Mrs MacLeod's
trial in Paris, which include a file of telegrams addressed
to Berlin which were secretly intercepted by a French
monitoring station and decoded. These decrypts, dated
between 13 December 1916 and 8 March 1917, were

introduced by the prosecution in July 1917 and, according to *Souvenirs*, the memoirs published in 1953 by her interrogator, Pierre Bouchardon, sealed Mata Hari's fate. Mata Hari's defence actually admitted her recruitment by 'von Kalle', insisting that she had made herself available to him on the instructions of a French intelligence officer. She also stated that 'von Kalle' had paid her 3,500 pesetas for being his mistress. The name of Wilhelm Canaris was never mentioned. Nevertheless, this omission did not prevent subsequent observers from muddying the waters further.

One such writer was the military historian Arch Whitehouse, who, in a previous volume, *Heroes and Legends of World War I*, had actually set about undermining some popular myths. His publishers, Doubleday, considered his book to be 'recounted with objectivity but also with great respect'.

But when Whitehouse described the case of Mrs MacLeod in *Espionage and Counterespionage*, he commented: 'In Madrid, Mata Hari renewed old acquaintances with the German Naval Attachés, Captain Canaris and Captain von Kalle, as well as the Military Attaché, Major von Kron; all three used espionage funds to pay for her services.'[4]

Whitehouse was evidently unaware that von Krohn had been a naval attaché and Canaris had not enjoyed any official or diplomatic standing at all. In any event Whitehouse was not the first to complicate Mata Hari's story. Even Sir Basil Thomson, the former Assistant Commissioner of the Metropolitan Police, confused his dates. As a brief diversion it is worth recounting some of the red herrings that a researcher tracing Mata Hari's movements is obliged to follow. Thomson's first volume of memoirs, *Queer People*, was released in 1922, and contained an account of his own meetings with Mrs

MacLeod. The two interviews had taken place in London after Mata Hari had been taken off the SS *Hollandia* in November 1916, and are confirmed by Scotland Yard's own records, but Sir Basil recalled that the French had,

on 25th July 1916 condemned her to death, but there was, as there usually is in such cases, an interminable delay, and it was not until 15 October that she was taken from Saint Lazare Prison to Vincennes for execution.[5]

His account advanced everything by twelve months and evidently confused later writers. To make matters worse, he misrepresented Mata Hari's first brief (but significant) stop-over in Madrid, which, of course, had taken place in mid-June 1916 while she was *en route* for Paris:

In July 1915 she was fulfilling a dancing engagement in Madrid, when information reached England that she had been consorting with members of the German Secret Service, and might be expected before long to be on her way back to Germany via Holland. This actually happened early in 1916. The ship put into Falmouth and she was brought ashore, together with her very large professional wardrobe, and escorted to London.[6]

In fact this incident happened on 13 November 1916 and Thomson was a year out. He was clearly mistaken about the dates on which he interviewed Mrs MacLeod, and in any event she was dancing in Paris, not Madrid, in July 1915. By combining Thomson's error of describing a non-existent journey from Madrid to Falmouth 'early in 1916' with the knowledge that Canaris was in Madrid from December 1915, it is easy to see how the confusion started. In subsequent years other authors attempted to follow Mata Hari's travels. In *Spy and Counter-Spy*, Richard Rowan became very disorientated and said of Mata Hari:

. . . tiring of the pretence of spying for France, she had set out for Spain via Holland and England. British port authorities, warned against her by their counter-espionage agents in the Netherlands, allowed her to land and proceed to London only upon the certainty that she would be invited to New Scotland Yard.[7]

Rowan has Mata Hari paying her (voluntary) visit to London while sailing from Holland to Spain, although we know that in reality she took the exact opposite route. When she landed in Falmouth she had actually been on her way back from Spain.

Four years after Rowan's contribution Hugh Cleland Hoy published his history of British naval intelligence in the Great War, *40 O.B.* In it Hoy reinterprets Mata Hari's journey from Madrid to Falmouth and back:

She was sent to Spain en route for Holland and Germany. From Vigo she sailed for Antwerp which was of course then occupied by the Germans. But a British patrol held up the ship in the English Channel and discovered her presence on board. Admiral Hall received a wireless message asking for instructions for dealing with this traveller. Now the Intelligence Department, though it knew nothing of Mata Hari's employment by France, did know a great deal about Mata Hari, and the fact that she was on her way to Germany tallied with our previous information about her. Admiral Hall therefore promptly replied by ordering Mata Hari to be brought into England and sent to Scotland Yard for interrogation.[8]

What makes Hoy's account so extraordinary is the fact that Thomson wrote the Foreword to it! In reality neither Hall nor Thomson had anything to do with Mata Hari's initial detention, which, of course, took place in Falmouth. According to Scotland Yard, Mrs MacLeod had been mistakenly identified as a German agent named Clara Benedict by the Special Branch officer on port security duty at Falmouth on 13 November 1916. This officer, George Grant, escorted her to London, where she was handed into the custody of Detective Chief Inspector Parker and lodged in Holloway Prison. Once she had been interviewed by Thomson and, belatedly, her true identity confirmed, she was moved to the Savoy Hotel before being placed on the next ship back to Spain.

Mata Hari's story is further complicated by one distinguished naval historian, Admiral Sir William James, who in 1955 wrote the biography of Admiral 'Blinker' Hall, the former Director of Naval Intelligence. Hall had been DNI during much of the Great War and one passage in *The Eyes of the Navy* is reminiscent of Thomson's original, faulty version. James places Hall as a participant in Thomson's interrogation of Mrs MacLeod and states that:

In July 1915 she was in Madrid, and it was known that she was consorting with members of the German secret service, so when the ship in which she was returning to Holland put in to Falmouth, early in 1916, she was taken ashore and brought to London for interrogation. Though Thomson and Hall were convinced that she was acting for the Germans and was on her way to Germany with information she had committed to memory, there was not enough evidence to detain her, and she was sent back to Spain.[9]

Having misrepresented his own encounter with Mrs MacLeod, Thomson seems to have authenticated James's version of the same incident. It would seem that there are an almost unlimited number of alternative explanations available to help keep alive a really durable myth. In the case of James and Thomson, both needed to substantiate the proposition that Mata Hari was engaged in espionage on behalf of the Germans (if not Canaris himself) before the incident of mistaken identity at Falmouth in November 1916.

The Mata Hari myth was perpetuated as recently as 1969 when Richard Deacon said of Canaris in *A History of the British Secret Service*: '. . . he was reputed to have paid Mata Hari to spy on the French and the Secret Service knew that in World War I he had worked against the allies in Madrid'.[10]

Although the possibility remains that Mrs MacLeod may have met Canaris between 12 and 14 June 1916, the odds seem to be heavily against it. The odds also seem to be against Stewart Menzies's involvement in this episode of Canaris's career, but that is also what some would have us believe. The story is neatly summed up in Robert Goldston's *Sinister Touches, The Secret War Against Hitler*, written in 1982:

Despite recurring bouts of malaria, Canaris proved so adept at finding out the routes of Allied Merchant ships that German U-boats in the Mediterranean began reaping a terrible harvest. British Intelligence took note and an officer from MI-6, a Captain Stewart Menzies, was sent to Spain to either capture or kill Canaris. But despite some incredibly narrow escapes, Canaris eluded Menzies, made his way back to Germany, and became a U-boat commander himself, eventually sinking some eighteen Allied ships in the Mediterranean. It was the first and only time the two future chiefs of their countries' intelligence services met in the field, but it was the beginning of a long and strange entanglement.[11]

Where did Goldston get the story? A clue can be found in his recommendation for further reading: Anthony Cave Brown's *Bodyguard of Lies*, published in 1976, and William Stevenson's *A Man Called Intrepid*, also published in 1976. He certainly seems to have acquired the Canaris-Menzies confrontation story from Cave Brown, who claimed: 'In the summer of 1916 Captain Menzies of MI-6 was sent to Spain to "kill or capture" the young German. It was to be their first and only encounter in the field.'[12]

Details of Menzies's mission are very sketchy and Cave Brown's references to it are limited to just four brief sentences. The first occurs after Canaris, armed with Chilean travel documents, had made his unsuccessful bid to return to Germany through Italy and Switzerland in February 1916. As we have seen, his escape from Italian custody enabled him to return to Madrid by the middle of the following month. Cave Brown attributes his escape to the intervention of Francisco Franco, who had apparently lobbied the Italian ambassador in Madrid for the German's freedom. Having avoided a firing squad, Canaris, according to Cave Brown, 'was back in Madrid in August of 1916 and Menzies quickly picked up his scent'.[13]

Still anxious to get to Berlin, Cave Brown suggests that Canaris arranged for a U-boat to come and pick him up.

The rendezvous was in Salitrona Bay off Cartagena. Pursued by Menzies and an Entente counterintelligence team, Canaris arrived there and took sanctuary aboard the interned German steamer Roma. Menzies soon found out where his quarry was hiding. His informant was Juan March, a young Jew who controlled the Cartagenan waterfront and who would come to control the economy of Spain. With the help of March, Menzies ringed Roma.

Under cover of darkness it is suggested that Canaris then slipped on to a Spanish fishing smack, part of the local mackerel fleet. The plan called for a rendezvous with a German submarine at sea. The U-boat commander would identify the vessel carrying Canaris because it would be flying a red pennant and flash the letter 'M' in Morse at the appointed time. Cave Brown writes that 'Menzies learned of his escape and signals were sent to the French submarines and surface vessels that were stationed along the line on which Canaris would rendezvous with the U-35.'

At exactly 0632 hours the German submarine surfaced in the midst of the fishing fleet, took Canaris and his two companions aboard, and promptly disappeared safely beneath the surface. The two French submarines, *Topaze* and *Opale*, were unaware of these events because they were submerged at the time, and 'although their periscopes were up, they had been blinded by the rays of the rising sun'.

For this entire episode, which is supposed to have taken place early in the morning of 1 October 1916, Cave Brown only mentions one source, a report written by Canaris 'to the Admirstab'. It seems to resemble Heinz Höhne's version of the same incident, the German edition of which had been published in Munich in 1976, the same year as *Bodyguard of Lies*. The English translation of Höhne's *Canaris* was not published until 1979.

There are two essential differences between the accounts given by Höhne and Cave Brown. The first is that Höhne omits any mention of Menzies. The second is that Höhne has relied on three sources: an article by Bodo Herzog in *Die Nachhut*, the newsletter of former Abwehr officers, of 8 January 1973, based on Canaris's own recollections; a report of the incident written by the commander of U-35 dated 21 October 1916; and the U-35's official War Diary. The three should be regarded as the only authentic accounts of Canaris's experiences in his escape from Spain in 1916. No other contemporary accounts have yet appeared.

In Höhne's version Canaris boarded a sailing boat to meet the U-boat, and had agreed a recognition signal of a red flag combined with the mainsail being dipped, but the rendezvous was betrayed by a French agent in the

German Embassy. The French, therefore, despatched the
Opale and an auxiliary cruiser disguised as a trawler.
When the trawler spotted Canaris's boat it approached,
found it to be crewed by Spaniards, and then lost interest.
Herzog put the following comments by Canaris in quo-
tation marks:

'The trawler quickly drew nearer. We hid in the sand ballast
inside the boat. The trawler hove to just astern of us and the
captain peered inside. Seeing only the Spanish crew, he slowly
proceeded south-east towards a vessel which was coming into
view there.'[14]

The U-35 surfaced in the lee of Canaris's boat, shielded
from the sight of the trawler by the sail, and took the
three passengers on board. By the time the trawler had
spotted the transfer and alerted the *Opale*, the German
submarine had slid back beneath the surface. Herzog
then quotes directly from Canaris again: 'We jumped
aboard at 0640. The entire manoeuvre took about three
or four minutes.'

Herzog's article of 1973 also quoted the *Opale*'s commander, Commandant Pradeau, who had placed the time
at 6 P.M. He had 'not noticed the boat because, seen from
my position, it was right in line with the setting sun,
which badly dazzled him'.

Apart from the obvious discrepancy about the timing,
the narrative is straightforward enough, if rather less
elaborate than Cave Brown's. However, a third version
was to appear in 1978 in David Kahn's *Hitler's Spies*. In
his, the recognition signal was the Morse K and a red
pennant. Kahn used Herzog's quotation from Canaris,
but without attribution:

The trawler came rapidly nearer. We hid ourselves in the
sand ballast inside the boat. The trawler stopped close by our

stern. Since it saw only the Spanish crew, it gradually continued
to travel southeast toward a vessel coming into sight there . . .[15]

Judging by the variety of different signals being dipped
and flashed by Canaris's boat, it seems astonishing that
the French vessel (with or without Menzies aboard) did
not take a closer interest!

All three versions of the same incident seem to have
enjoyed the same origins, but Cave Brown's account is
unique in respect of his insertion of Menzies. In other
words, Herzog's article was the first publication to draw
attention to the circumstances of Canaris's escape.
Höhne's *Canaris* followed three years later, but only
Cave Brown's contribution makes the controversial link
between Canaris and Menzies. Certainly there is nothing
in any of the German documents to support the story.

The British contribution to the affair is difficult to
trace. Menzies was transferred away from his regiment to
intelligence duties at the British Expeditionary Force's
headquarters at Montreuil on 18 December 1915 and
was, in theory at least, available to undertake secret
missions into neutral Spain. However, various accounts
of GHQ's work at Montreuil and Beaumerie, including
the published memoirs of at least one senior Staff officer,
Sir James Marshall-Cornwall (*War and Rumours of War*),
places Menzies in France, not Spain. One is tempted to
wonder why the British needed to send Captain Menzies
to Cartagena when it is known that there was already a
flourishing network of Allied agents at work there, not
the least of whom was the novelist A. E. W. Mason.
Mason patrolled the Spanish coast on a steam yacht on
behalf of the Naval Intelligence Division and his adventures (which include a confrontation with a German
U-boat refuelling in Cartagena harbour) are well documented. One of his stories was published in the American

Metropolitan Magazine as early as March 1916, when he was still active in the area. In any event the Menzies-Canaris encounter now seems to be uncheckable: Menzies himself died in 1968 and Juan March died in 1962. It is such a vacuum that enables a myth to survive and develop, and that is exactly what happened with the Menzies-Canaris relationship. Is such scepticism justified? One passage in particular in *Bodyguard of Lies* tends to undermine the reader's faith in Cave Brown. While discussing Menzies and Canaris's alleged opposition to Hitler at the outset of the Second World War, he suggests that the question of whether or not Canaris could be trusted to work with MI6 against Hitler was debated and that 'These questions deeply divided the small group of officers in command of MI-6. As one would write . . .'[16] Cave Brown then proceeds to quote a ten-line extract from *A History of the British Secret Service* by Richard Deacon. But far from ever having been an MI6 officer, Deacon is in reality Donald McCormick, a former Foreign Manager of the *Sunday Times*.

The question of Canaris's loyalties during the Second World War was first raised by Ian Colvin in 1951, two years after the publication of Karl Heinz Abshagen's definitive biography, *Canaris*. Colvin's book, *Canaris: Chief of Intelligence*, was highly controversial for it suggested, for the first time, that Canaris might have been a British spy. The dust-jacket posed the question: Was the head of Hitler's secret service really a British agent?

The question naturally had all kinds of implications for military historians and there was, therefore, considerable interest in Colvin's account. His own background was that of a foreign correspondent, married to a former MI6 secretary. He had been posted to Berlin before the war and had reported on events for a number of Fleet Street newspapers, including the *News Chronicle*. But Colvin had not got on the track of Canaris in the German capital. According to his own account, he had learned of the story in England, after the war:

I was casting these questions over one of the Under-Secretaries of State at lunch when the German wars were over and he rose to the subject, remarking with a certain emphasis: 'Well, our Intelligence was not badly equipped. As you know, we had Admiral Canaris, and that was a considerable thing.'[17]

In spite of this apparently well-informed source, Colvin made little progress in finding the answer to his own question. As the former CIA officer, George Constantinides, commented in his masterly work of analysis, *Intelligence and Espionage: An Analytical Bibliography*: 'Colvin left the answer to the judgement of the reader.'[18]

Colvin was certainly aware of the improbability of Canaris having been a British agent. As he himself admitted:

Although I had occasion over a number of years, as a correspondent of British newspapers in Berlin, to catch glimpses of the workings of the Chief of Intelligence Services of the German Armed Forces, it would have no more occurred to me to describe him as a British agent than I would have described Talleyrand as an agent of Castlereagh.

This honest qualification did not prevent subsequent observers from exaggerating and misrepresenting Colvin's position. Herbert Molloy Mason's *To Kill The Devil* referred to Colvin as 'a friend and confidant of Admiral Canaris'.[19]

Six years later Colvin returned to the subject in his revised edition of *Canaris: Chief of Intelligence* for Pan paperbacks, now newly entitled *Canaris: Hitler's Secret Enemy*. In a new preface the author identified his original source: 'Sir Christopher Warner, the late Under-Secretary in the Foreign Office, whose chance remark at the table started me on the theme of this book, died while this Pan edition was being prepared.'[20]

The identification of Sir Christopher Warner as Colvin's source was an illuminating development. At the time of the publication of *Canaris: Chief of Intelligence*, Warner was the British ambassador to Belgium and was at the height of his distinguished Foreign Service career. Unfortunately, Warner was unable to corroborate Colvin's statement as he was dead. There remains some doubt about whether Warner really gave Colvin the information because he was later to identify Menzies himself as his original source. Only at that time Menzies, too, was conveniently dead.

In 1969 Group Captain F. W. Winterbotham, the former head of MI6's Air Section, published his memoirs, entitled *Secret and Personal*. Although Winterbotham is now well-known as the man who 'blew' the ULTRA secret, this event did not take place until 1974. In his first book, five years earlier, Winterbotham studiously avoided any mention of such contentious issues as code-breaking or Bletchley. Nevertheless, he did recall that it had still been possible to contact the enemy through agents in Madrid and Lisbon in 1942 although 'it was a little surprising when Canaris made an approach to his opposite number my own chief'.[21]

Winterbotham remembered that 'Canaris proposed to stop hostilities by the elimination of Hitler and the Nazis'. But, for reasons that remain unclear, 'In the event the contact with Canaris came to nothing.'

Winterbotham failed to elaborate further about this abortive attempt to link up with Menzies, and certainly none of those surviving senior MI6 officers who served in Lisbon or Madrid admit any knowledge of the affair. While the apparent intention of Canaris to reach the

Allies is strengthened by Winterbotham, an authoritative inside source, little of substance had been added to the debate. Despite this dearth of corroboration, Winterbotham's reference was to become oft-repeated. In the same year, 1969, Richard Deacon, for example, said that Menzies had been in a position to open direct negotiations with Canaris in 1942. 'Menzies had no illusions about Canaris: he realized that the Admiral's chief concern was to preserve German power intact as a price for helping to end the war.'[22]

Describing how the approach had come to nothing, Deacon actually quoted the taciturn Menzies as being thwarted in certain Foreign Office quarters 'for fear of offending Russia'.

The matter of Canaris's loyalty needed to be resolved and in 1970 the French journalist André Brissaud returned to the subject in his biography, *Canaris*. An English edition was subsequently published three years later by Weidenfeld & Nicolson and, coincidentally, Ian Colvin was employed as the principal translator. This was an extraordinary development, especially since Brissaud rejected Colvin's 'British agent' idea, referring to it as 'a theory which everybody who has read the present book so far will discard, sharing my conviction that Canaris never worked for the Allied Secret Services'.[23]

Colvin accepted this criticism and took the opportunity to explain his position further in an introduction to Brissaud's English edition. He began by describing how his original question concerning Canaris's loyalties found its way on to the dust-jacket:

My own biographical study of Canaris, *Chief of Intelligence*, so excited the publisher, Victor Gollancz, that he asked the rhetorical question on the dust-jacket whether he had acted for the British – was he a British agent? André Brissaud evidently disapproves of such an eye-catching interpretation of the man; for Canaris, though a proven enemy of the Nazi regime, was no common spy, no double agent and in his high position orchestrated the score rather than peddled secrets himself.[24]

This statement should not be interpreted as Colvin apologizing for Gollancz's 'rhetorical question', because he went on to authenticate the theory by identifying a new source for his information:

We shall never be told how close at times the contact was between Canaris himself and the British Chief of Intelligence; but I am able to add here a detail, unrevealed in my own book twenty years ago, as it was still too sensitive then for publication. Major-General Sir Stuart [*sic*] Menzies, the wartime Head of British Intelligence, to whom in his Westminster office in October 1942 I explained my theory that his opposite number in Germany was in reality working against Hitler with the object of shortening the war, interrupted the conversation, saying with a smile: 'I think I know what is going on in his mind. Would you like to meet Canaris?'

It would now seem that Sir Christopher Warner was not the first person to tell Colvin about Canaris. It was Sir Stewart Menzies. This seems unlikely, although Colvin's inability to spell Sir Stewart's Christian name does not necessarily undermine the truth of this claim, but once again the quoted source, Menzies, had died the previous year, in June 1968, and was therefore unable to comment. Colvin directly quoted his supposed conversation with Menzies:

. . . when I declared myself ready to meet the Admiral, General Menzies went on to say: 'I should have to send a more senior man with you. You would not mind that? I don't doubt your capability, but you are a young man and I would wish him to think that I was taking him seriously.' The matter was left that Sir Stuart required a week or two to obtain official approval for myself and one of his staff to meet Canaris.

According to Colvin, the plan was called off because of official opposition. Menzies is alleged to have explained that 'we have to be very careful not to offend the Russians'. That Menzies should have asked a young newspaperman to participate in such a delicate and significant meeting seems somewhat improbable, but it was not long before another author developed the idea further by suggesting that Menzies and Canaris rendezvoused together in Spain in 1943.

This extraordinary revelation was made by Heinz Höhne in his massive study, *Canaris*. In Höhne's version Canaris and Menzies actually met in Spain:

> By summer 1943 the Abwehr chief had gained his first objective. General Menzies and Donovan intimated to their German counterpart that they were prepared to meet him in Spain, and the three secret service chiefs convened at Santander soon afterwards.[26]

This was the first occasion that anyone had suggested that Menzies had encountered Canaris face to face. The inclusion of General Bill Donovan, the head of the American Office of Strategic Services (OSS), added yet another dimension to an already odd story. Höhne revealed that his source was a former Abwehr officer, F. Justus von Einem, who claimed to have attended the meeting as a member of Canaris's personal staff. Judging by Höhne's faith in his informant, von Einem enjoyed the unique position of being privy to deliberations of both the White House and the Foreign Office, for von Einem is credited as the source for the following statement: 'Roosevelt called his presumptuous OSS chief to heel and the head of the SIS took pains to minimize the significance of his forbidden trip to Spain *vis-à-vis* the British Foreign Office.'[27]

The story of the 'surreptitious flirtation with Allied

representatives' has now escalated to a conflict between Roosevelt and Donovan, and Menzies and the Foreign Office. Is this plausible? It is certainly not borne out by wartime documents or the recollection of colleagues of the two Allied chiefs. Although little has been written about Menzies, no less than four major biographies have been published about General 'Wild Bill' Donovan. Only Anthony Cave Brown's *The Last Hero* supports the theory of a Canaris-Donovan meeting, but his evidence is contradictory. Cave Brown refers to a post-war letter from Canaris's widow as evidence:

It is evident that Canaris and Donovan did meet. It is not possible to say when or where they met, but a personal letter from Frau Canaris to Donovan in 1946 certainly suggests association between Canaris and Donovan and it is known that immediately after World War II Donovan sought out Frau Canaris, made life easier for her with a financial grant, and made her welcome at the villa at Dahlem, Berlin, which he and his service occupied.[28]

The content of the single letter cited by Cave Brown does nothing to suggest that a meeting between Canaris and Donovan took place. Apparently Cave Brown felt that the mere existence of a letter was at least part proof that a meeting had taken place. After all, what else would explain Donovan's generosity to the widow of a vanquished enemy? In another, later chapter of the same book Cave Brown refers to the same letter from Frau Canaris to Donovan (dating it '15 November 1945') in which she thanked Donovan for his kindness for providing her with some unexpected comforts. Cave Brown also describes Donovan's motivation: 'WJD felt that Frau Canaris might know where there were copies of Canaris's diaries, which might show evidence of, or lead to, the conspiracy theory.'[29]

Cave Brown then explains the circumstances of OSS's hunt for Frau Canaris, who

was not located before October or November 1945, when Norden and Muller found her in desperate straits with her daughters in the beautiful little village of Niederau, one of the steamer stops on the Ammersee, near Munich. Frau Canaris received Muller, whom she knew, and Norden, and at WJD's instructions certain gifts were sent to the Canaris family – probably money, food and comforts.[30]

It would certainly seem plausible that Donovan's motives for helping Frau Canaris are correctly portrayed by Cave Brown, but by transposing the date of her letter of thanks from 1945 to 1946 the author has created his own evidence of a non-existent Canaris-Donovan meeting. Indeed, Cave Brown admits in a separate chapter:

. . . there were rumours in the OSS that Donovan and Canaris met personally in Spain in March or April 1943 and again in Istanbul in the late summer or early fall of 1943. But we do not know if these meetings actually took place and, if they did, what transpired.[31]

Cave Brown's position has therefore been presented extremely ambiguously. In one chapter 'it is evident' that Canaris and Donovan did meet, while in another he expresses doubt that any meetings actually took place.

Richard Dunlop's equally lengthy biography of Donovan, *America's Master Spy*, reported that 'Admiral Wilhelm Canaris, German intelligence chief during World War II, once remarked that of all the Allied leaders, he most would have liked to meet and know William J. Donovan.'[32] This idea is unsupported by any source reference, but such a comment would have to have been made between Donovan's appointment as head of OSS in

June 1942 and Canaris's execution in April 1945, which implies the existence of an extraordinarily well-placed source. Assuming that the remark is correctly reported, it gives the impression that Canaris's ambition was unfulfilled.

Such a conclusion does not preclude a meeting between Menzies and Canaris; yet, as we have seen, the evidence available is slim. What started out as Winterbotham's 'approach' in the context of a neutral country quickly became Deacon's 'direct negotiations'. Thereafter it was established as a myth and was further embellished by Höhne, who included Donovan in the act.

If no meeting took place, what then is the explanation for Canaris's behaviour? Was he merely a secret sympathizer with the Allies, or was he one of the rather more active anti-Nazis? Paul Leverkühn, who was Canaris's wartime representative in Istanbul, made his view known in *German Military Intelligence*, which was, incidentally, translated by Constantine FitzGibbon and R. H. Stevens (the latter being a former SIS officer of some notoriety): 'Nor have I any reason to believe that Canaris at any time sought or made contact with Germany's enemies, though frequent opportunities for such activity were presented to him.'[33]

In his massive volume *Hitler's Spies*, the American historian David Kahn agreed: 'Even though his secret agency afforded him innumerable opportunities, he never conspired to kill Hitler, or even depose him. (At most he sheltered some resistance people.) He never betrayed secrets to the Allies.'[34]

This view was not shared by Pierre Galante in *Operation Valkyrie*. He insisted that Canaris had played a critical role in more than one plot to kill Hitler. The first had taken place in September 1938, when 'Canaris had prepared a kind of manifesto addressed to the German people, a complete exposé of the crimes of the Nazis'.[35]

In another conspiracy, which had been aborted in September 1943, 'Admiral Canaris provided a plane for the Berlin conspirators'.[36]

Hans von Herwarth, who actually took part in the 20 July attempt on Hitler's life, commented in *Against Two Evils*: 'A figure who was central to the work of the Resistance was Admiral Wilhelm Canaris. Over a period of years, this man quietly worked to protect the organization against the danger of counter-attack by Himmler.'[37]

The contrast in opinions about this single man could hardly be greater. Some believed him simply to have been a passive spectator. Others portrayed him as one of Germany's leading anti-Nazis and even an Allied agent. What is the truth?

Paradoxically, it was Ian Colvin who was the first to come close to unravelling the mystery surrounding Canaris's illicit wartime activities. In 1951, in his book *Canaris: Chief of Intelligence*, Colvin recounted how a Polish diplomat had taken him to visit a lady whom he referred to as 'Madame J'. She was, at the time he was researching his subject, living in a small house in Surrey. Colvin recalled:

First she gave us tea and when I had asked her whether she had known Canaris she ran on from memory. 'If I ask you not to mention my name or tell anything that would identify me, it is because I do not often tell this story and would prefer to tell it once and have done with it. My husband and I lived in Berlin before the war. We knew the Polish colony there and had some contact with the Germans. I remember meeting some of the German generals in the house of our military attaché.'[38]

Like the good journalist that he was, Colvin had protected his source even in the space of these brief sentences. Her story was quite remarkable because she insisted that she had acted as a link between the British and Canaris. She remembered how her acquaintance with Canaris stirred both the Polish and British authorities in wartime Switzerland: 'When she mentioned this name again, the Poles showed immediate interest and the British reacted, too. They wanted to hear more about him. Madame J stayed in Switzerland.'[39]

She had no doubt that she had been working for the British Secret Service and described her covert meetings with Canaris in neutral Berne:

'At times the tension in him affected me deeply when he spoke of their aims against Hitler. I asked the British sometimes – "Shall I tell him to go ahead?"; the British were very correct in such matters and said nothing. But the British Secret Service could keep secrets, and throughout the war this link was undiscovered.'[40]

Perhaps even more extraordinary than her story was Colvin's treatment of it. The interview with 'Madame J' is abruptly concluded and he makes no further reference to it. If his source was to be believed, why the rhetorical question? There is no obvious explanation in *Canaris: Chief of Intelligence*, so one is bound to conclude that the author was not prepared to commit himself entirely. The story was evidently disbelieved by Canaris's subsequent biographers because none refer to the mysterious 'Madame J'.

In 1981, while pursuing various other strands of wartime intelligence operations in Switzerland, I chanced across a retired SIS officer who had served in Berne immediately after the war. Although he had difficulty remembering her name, he was adamant that 'the wife of the former Polish military attaché in Berlin had been our link with Canaris'. I then discovered that the Polish military attaché would have been Colonel Antoni Szymanski and that his wife's name was Halina. Intrigued, I traced a member of the wartime SIS Station in Berne and heard about the agent who had been known to him only as 'agent Z-5/1'. So after more than forty years it was established, once and for all, that Canaris had kept in touch with SIS during the war, using a displaced Polish lady as a conduit. During the summer of 1983 I traced Halina Szymanska to her grandson's home in Mobile, Alabama, and visited her there. Although she was then seventy-seven years old, she was able to recall many of her wartime experiences and her meetings with Canaris.

When details of Madame Szymanska's full story, with her real name, appeared in my book *MI6: British Secret Intelligence Service Operations 1909–45*, two *Sunday Times* journalists, Barrie Penrose and Simon Freeman, contacted a retired career SIS officer, Andrew King, who had been privy to details of her case:

We have spoken to Andrew King who was an MI6 officer in Switzerland at the same time. He told us that Canaris had tipped off Szymanska in the late autumn of 1940 about Hitler's plans to invade Russia the following year. He says that Canaris and Szymanska had an unspoken understanding that this information would be relayed to London.[41]

For the first time, an SIS source had 'gone on the record' and confirmed that Canaris had deliberately passed important strategic intelligence to the Allies, albeit via an 'unspoken understanding'. King's own career in SIS spanned nearly thirty years and included postings in Vienna and Hong Kong, as well as his role in Switzerland. Hardly an unreliable witness, and his testimony more than anyone else's has helped, for once, to prove the truth of what had been regarded by many as just another wartime intelligence myth.

3

The Agent from Orkney

'Alfred Wehring' never existed and the whole account is an unedifying journalistic invention.

HARALD BÜSCH in *U-Boats at War*

Alfred Wahring [*sic*], a naval officer in the First World War, gave the British a disaster which nearly brought down the government. As a naturalized British citizen under the name of Albert Oertel, a Swiss, Wahring operated a watch-repair business in Kirkwall in the Orkney Islands, within sight of Scapa Flow. He observed one of Britain's premier warships, the huge *Royal Oak*, enter the protected roadstead without having to wait until the submarine nets were lowered, which meant the ship was vulnerable from the east.

LAURAN PAINE in *The Abwehr*

The Second World War was not yet six weeks old when HMS *Royal Oak* was sunk in the British Home Fleet's supposedly safe, impregnable anchorage at Scapa Flow on Saturday, 14 October 1939, with the loss of 833 lives. A small explosion vibrated through the battleship at four minutes past one in the morning, and was followed, twelve minutes later, by a second, catastrophic explosion. By half-past one the *Royal Oak* had capsized with massive loss of life. No 'Abandon Ship' order had been given because of a power failure. Many of those on board, including the captain, had thought the fatal explosion had been internal and had ignited in the ship's Inflammable Store, but the Naval Intelligence Division disputed this. They reported that a news item broadcast on German radio, intercepted by the BBC's monitoring service at

Caversham Park, claimed that a lone U-boat had been responsible for the sinking. Was this Nazi propaganda or the truth? An Admiralty Board of Enquiry, headed by Lord Chatfield, a former First Sea Lord, was hastily empanelled to investigate. The Board concluded that the German version was probably true, and decided that a single U-boat had somehow manoeuvred itself into the anchorage and had torpedoed the battleship. The Enquiry pinpointed a number of lapses in the local defences which might have enabled an enemy submarine to carry out its mission undetected. Furthermore, they found no evidence to support the then popular theory of a sabotage conspiracy.

That the *Royal Oak* had been sunk by a torpedo fired from a single U-boat operating alone was confirmed by the Germans themselves when, on 18 October 1939, Captain Gunther Prien, commander of U-47, was introduced to representatives of the world's newspapers at a press conference in Berlin. William Shirer was there, and he recorded the event in his *Berlin Diary*:

> Prien told us little of how he did it. He said he had no trouble getting past the boom protecting the bay. I got the impression, though he said nothing to justify it, that he must have followed a British craft, perhaps a minesweeper, into the base. British negligence must have been something terrific.[1]

According to the claims made at the Nazi Propaganda Ministry, Prien had succeeded where others had failed. In the First World War two German U-boats, commanded by Kapitans von Henning and Emsmann, had been sunk whilst attempting the same operation. U-47 had pulled off the impossible and, alone, had penetrated Scapa's famous defences. Many newspapers carried stories of Prien's press conference, and the Board of Enquiry made an examination of three English-language reports. The

Board concluded that Prien's reported statements were probably correct, and that the *Royal Oak* had indeed been sunk by a German torpedo. Prien's own account, *I Sank the 'Royal Oak'*, was published in Berlin in 1940, but post-war investigators were unable to cross-examine him. He was presumed lost on 8 March 1941 with the U-47, which is thought to have been sunk by the destroyer HMS *Wolverine*. Nevertheless, his account has largely been substantiated by the U-47's War Diary and Admiral Doenitz's recollections in *The Phantom of Scapa Flow* by Alexandre Korganoff.[2] In addition one of Prien's brother officers, Wolfgang Frank, wrote his biography *Enemy Submarine* using Prien's own diaries which documented the attack.

Nobody doubted that Prien had entered Scapa Flow in his U-boat and sunk the *Royal Oak*, but there was much speculation about how he had achieved this feat. As the point was talked about and discussed, many suggestions were put forward until a myth grew up that he must have had help from the shore. Did a spy guide him?

This suggestion first appeared in print on 16 May 1942 in an article entitled 'U-Boat Espionage' in the American journal, the *Saturday Evening Post*, written by Curt Riess. Riess himself was a political exile from his native Austria and had made his reputation writing about intelligence matters. In October 1941 he had published *Total Espionage*, a detailed account of Nazi activities around the world. According to Riess, the U-boat that had sunk the *Royal Oak* had been guided past the obstacles surrounding the Home Fleet's anchorage by a German spy who, before the war, had posed as a Swiss watchmaker in the nearest town to Scapa Flow, Kirkwall: 'The man, whose last name begins with a W, was neither a Swiss nor a watchmaker, but a German lieutenant commander working for the German U-boat Espionage.' This unnamed

spy had discovered, 'on October 11, 1939', that two
entrances to Scapa Flow had not yet been fitted with
modern submarine nets. Accordingly he sent a coded
message to The Hague and, two days later, kept a
rendezvous with a U-boat and guided it into the anchorage. Riess also claimed that these events were known to
the Royal Navy: 'The naval inquiry board in London had
little difficulty in finding out that watchmaker W had
disappeared. His deserted car was found the morning
after the sinking in the vicinity of Scapa Flow.' This
remarkable story is not supported by secret papers docu-
menting the Enquiry's deliberations which have recently
been released by the Public Record Office.[3] Nevertheless,
the article was accompanied by a wealth of impressive
detail, including the name of Wilhelm Canaris, the Chief
of the Abwehr, whose identity was still a secret in 1942.
It was followed up three years later by another American
newspaper journalist, Kurt Singer, who wrote a chapter
in his book *Spies and Traitors in World War II* entitled
'The Man Who Really Sank the Royal Oak'. Singer had
also been born in Austria and had written well-received
biographies of Hermann Goering and Pastor Niemoller.
Of his sources for his book Singer said:

I have concerned myself with matters of espionage since 1933.
I actively participated in exposing Axis agents, and I have
had the honor of being consulted by Allied military and civilian governmental agents. Ninety-five per cent of the names
and incidents mentioned in this book are taken from well-
substantiated documents.[4]

The man referred to as W by Riess was, according to
Singer, really named Alfred Wehring. In 1927 he had
taken up the Swiss identity of Albert Oertel and had
moved to the Orkney Islands. Ten years later he
had become a naturalized British subject. Having studied

the local defences for more than a decade 'Oertel' was in an ideal position to act as a pilot for a submarine raider. In 1939 he signalled to Germany on his secret transmitter and apparently kept a rendezvous with the U-boat at Kirk Sound, equipped with up-to-date charts marked with the positions of the most recently placed British block-ships. Together 'Oertel' and the U-boat skipper, Gunther Prien, slipped past the obstructions and made a torpedo approach on the *Royal Oak*. Once the attack had been successfully executed Prien made his way back to a hero's welcome at Kiel.

Singer confirmed most of the account given by Riess and gave a detailed description of 'Oertel's' mission and his biographical background: 'Alfred Wehring was one of the youngest captains in Germany. He had proved himself an able officer of the battleship *Admiral Hipper*.'[5] Apparently Wehring had been recruited as a spy when 'in 1923 Canaris on his own initiative sent out Germany's first naval spy since the Versailles Treaty had been signed'. Wehring evidently turned out to be an outstanding spy:

Canaris had a high opinion of his abilities, and in 1923 chose Wehring for the important new appointment. Wehring was to become a salesman for a German watch firm. A respectable representative of a harmless firm, he would visit many countries of Europe, in all of which he was to keep alert to new naval constructions. After three years of this, Wehring was sent to Switzerland, where he apprenticed himself to a Swiss watchmaking concern and made himself into a proficient watchmaker. In 1927 he emigrated to England . . . He settled in Kirkwall on the Orkney Islands, close to the Scapa Flow base.[6]

Having outlined Wehring's career, Singer described how he had masterminded the raid:

But the facts are positive. A month after the outbreak of war, Ortel [*sic*] learned that the traps and nets on the eastern approaches to Scapa Flow were not in place. They had been inspected and found to be unsound, weakened by water-rot and the gnawing of wood borers.[7]

Having discovered the weakness of the defences Wehring sent a radio message to 'the German naval attaché in Holland, Baron von Bulow':[8] 'From The Hague the message was speedily forwarded to Canaris, who learned the essential fact that invulnerable Scapa Flow was in actuality defenceless and wide open to any submarine attack. A few days would elapse before the defences were replaced.'[9]

The rest of the operation was relatively straightforward: 'Captain Gunther Prien of the Submarine B-06 was singled out to execute the plan.' Prien kept a prearranged rendezvous with Wehring 'close to the easternmost tip of Pomona Island' and despatched a rubber dinghy to collect the spy. 'Ortel handed over his data. He had prepared naval maps, with a complete diagramming of every yard of Scapa Flow. He pointed out where the defenceless parts lay.' Once the submarine had completed the attack it made its escape and set a course for Kiel with Wehring on board. Singer says of the return to its home port:

In the midst of the celebration, one man not in uniform slipped away from the dock to which submarine B-06 was moored. Though the newspapers gave citations to everyone of the crew by name, not a word was said about this civilian. The man had not been invited to the banquet.[10]

In 1955 Singer published a further volume, *More Spy Stories*, and reproduced much of his original material in a chapter entitled 'The Man Who Sank the Royal Oak'. Obviously his faith in the original story had not been shaken in the intervening decade, for he repeats the story with added conviction: 'Though the newspapers gave citations to every one of the crew by name, not a word was said about the civilian. Yet this was the brilliant spy who was really responsible for the successful attack on Scapa Flow.'[11]

Although Singer's version had remained unchanged, a newcomer had taken up the tale. In 1947 a former Czech resistance fighter named Edward Spiro published *Secrets of the British Secret Service* under the pen-name E. H. Cookridge. He related how, in 1927, 'a Dutch citizen, Mijnheer Joachim Van Schullerman, arrived in England, as the representative of a Swiss firm of watchmakers and jewellers'. The Dutchman opened a workshop in Kirkwall in 1928 and

> By 1932, as he had been a resident for five years in Britain, Schullerman applied to the Scottish Office for naturalization. Everyone in Kirkwall knew him well, and it was not difficult to find a few leading citizens to vouch for him. The papers went through without a hitch.[12]

In fact, according to Cookridge, Schullerman was in reality Kapitan Kurt von Mueller:

> Knight of the Iron Cross, Knight of the Military Merit Order personally awarded by the Kaiser for gallantry at the Battles of Jutland and the Kattegat, he had endured the shame of watching the defeated German navy sail into surrender at Scapa Flow in 1918.[13]

Von Mueller's career had begun when 'In 1917 he happened to be in Spain, at the same time as Canaris while the latter recuperated from his labours as Von Papen's agent in America. The two struck up a friendship which was periodically refreshed by occasional meetings.' Von Mueller's similarity to Wehring is remarkable, even down to a visit to Switzerland, where 'to make some money he got a job with a firm at La Chaux de Fonds and learned watchmaking'.[14] Von Mueller then combined espionage with watchmaking in the Orkneys, and Cookridge admits: 'How Von Mueller had pieced together the information of the intricate booms and nets of Scapa Flow's anti-submarine defences probably will remain a mystery.'[15]

Nevertheless, the spy succeeded and 'On 14 October he somehow secured a small boat and made his way past the coastguard defences to keep the rendezvous with the U-boat six miles to the east of Scapa.'[16] The story includes the mandatory celebration:

> In Kiel a great celebration was held as the submarine entered the dock. Admiral Doenitz was there to congratulate the captain and crew. Few people bothered about the short, stoutish man in civilian clothes who unobtrusively emerged from the conning tower and hurried to a waiting aeroplane which took off for Berlin.[17]

Astonishingly, Cookridge had prefaced his book with these remarks:

> I have tried to avoid false romanticism in this account. Fiction may sometimes be more entertaining, and readers who take their ideas about espionage work from adventure novels may be disappointed. But I thought it better to rely upon careful investigation and official documents rather than vivid imagination.[18]

It did not take the newspapers long to follow up Cookridge's story. On 24 December 1947 a French-controlled paper in Berlin, *Der Kurier*, confirmed that Alfred Wehring 'had distinguished himself in the First World War as one of the youngest German naval captains on the battleship *Admiral Hipper*'.

More than a year after these words had been published the *Saturday Evening Post* returned to the subject in August 1949 in an article entitled 'The U-Boat Mystery of Scapa Flow', in which Burke Wilkinson described 'a subplot, often hinted at, widely distorted'. It was, of course, about 'a certain Alfred Wehring, a German naval officer with a fine World War I record'. Wilkinson disclosed that Wehring had adopted the 'typically Swiss name of Albert Oertel' and 'in 1932 Albert Oertel became a British subject'. Some of the details have a familiar ring to them:

Wehring next turned up in Switzerland, apprenticed to a Swiss watch company. He learned his trade thoroughly and soon became an expert craftsman. In 1927 he emigrated to England, equipped with a shiny new passport thoughtfully provided by Admiral Canaris. Alfred Wehring now answered to the typically Swiss name of Albert Oertel.

The only difference between Wilkinson's account and previous versions lay in the date of Oertel's naturalization. He gave the date as 1932, the same as Cookridge's Dutchman, but Riess had made it five years later, in 1937.

In 1956 another book, *The Labyrinth*, confirmed the part played by Wehring in the sinking of the *Royal Oak*. On this occasion the author was Walter Schellenberg, formerly the head of the Sicherheitsdienst (SD). At the end of the war Schellenberg had taken refuge in Sweden, but in June 1945 he had been deported to Germany to stand trial for war crimes. He had been interrogated by the British for nineteen months and had eventually been charged with war crimes at Nuremberg in January 1948. In April 1949 he had been sentenced to six years' imprisonment, but he had only served two years because of the time he had already spent in custody. He had been released in June 1951 and had died in Turin in March 1952. His posthumously published autobiography was authenticated by the distinguished academic and historian, Alan (now Lord) Bullock, who stated in the introduction: 'All these are episodes not from fiction but from the history of the last twenty years and they are described by the man who became the head of Hitler's Foreign Intelligence Service.'[19] He went on to say: 'I believe that Schellenberg's memoirs, quite apart from the interest of the narrative, have considerable value as historical evidence.'[20] Schellenberg's account of Wehring's contribution almost exactly followed those given by Riess and Singer:

How important intelligently planned long-range preparatory work can be – and how rewarding in the end – is shown by the successful operation of the German U-boat Commander, Captain Prien, against the British naval base at Scapa Flow in October 1940. The success of this operation was made possible by careful preparatory work over a period of fifteen years. Alfred Wehring had been a Captain in the German Imperial Navy and later joined the military sector of the Secret Service. After the First World War he became a traveller for a German watch factory. Working all the time under orders from the Secret Service, he learned the watchmaker's trade thoroughly in Switzerland. In 1927, under the name of Albert Oertel and with a Swiss passport, he settled in England. In 1932 he became a naturalized British subject, and soon afterwards opened a small jewellery shop at Kirkwall in the Orkneys, near Scapa Flow, whence from time to time he sent us reports on the movements of the British Home Fleet.

It was in the beginning of October 1939, that he sent us the important information that the eastern approach to Scapa Flow through the Kierkesund was not closed off by anti-submarine nets but only by hulks lying relatively far apart. On receipt of this information Admiral Doenitz ordered Captain Prien to attack any British warships in Scapa Flow.[21]

Schellenberg's reference to Alfred Wehring and the fact that 'he sent us the important information' implied that the case had been known to the SD Chief. As we shall see later, there is every chance that Schellenberg first learned of Wehring's existence from the British, and not from his own experience.

Schellenberg's memoirs were followed by the first significant independent investigation of the Scapa Flow disaster. In 1959 Alexander McKee published his conclusions in *Black Saturday*. He was adamant that Wehring had never existed and, furthermore, he suggested that Prien's submarine had never penetrated Scapa Flow. Certainly Prien's own autobiography had contained several inaccuracies, probably as a result of some heavy-handed wartime censorship, as might be expected in Germany in 1940. Naturally, it omitted any mention of Wehring's role. In 1958 Prien's commander, Admiral Karl Doenitz, released his memoirs. Although he confirmed that Prien's U-47 had been the submarine responsible for torpedoing the *Royal Oak*, he too denied any knowledge of Wehring. Doenitz insisted that he had planned the raid with photographic intelligence obtained by the Luftwaffe. Now McKee undermined the entire episode.

The story was further complicated in March 1963 by John Bulloch's history of *MI5*, the British Security Service. Bulloch had succeeded in gaining access to an unpublished manuscript written by Lady Kell, the widow of Major-General Sir Vernon Kell, MI5's first Director-General. According to his account, which was in part based on Lady Kell's manuscript, Sir Vernon had been held responsible for the lapse in security at Scapa Flow:

It was obvious that the Germans had been supplied with up-to-date information by a spy. And as there had been no aerial reconnaissance before the submarine had got in, it was equally obvious that the spy had been able to send to Germany the message that the *Royal Oak* was in the anchorage within a day of her arrival.[22]

The implication of Bulloch's version was that MI5 themselves had believed that a German spy had been responsible for the disaster. MI5's opinion had apparently been shared by others:

MI5, Naval Security, the Special Branch and police all went into action to try to find the man who had made the German exploit possible. They all failed. This was a serious defeat for British security, and a great blow to Kell, whose confidence that he had rounded up all the German agents in Britain was so quickly shattered.

That the Security Service had taken the spy theory seriously was later confirmed in 1971 by Ladislas Farago in *Game of the Foxes*, who stated that the British authorities had indeed checked the original *Saturday Evening Post* story, 'by the simple process of an MI5 agent in New York interviewing the inventor, and accepting his veracity at face value'.[23]

Could Schellenberg have acquired his version of events from a British source during his many post-war interrogations by MI5? The possibility seems increasingly likely given the apparent British belief in it. Either way, Bulloch's contribution marked a milestone in the development of the Scapa Flow myth. The story, having originated in America, had been repeated by a Nazi espionage chief and had been accepted by the British. In fact the tale went full circle in 1963, for a recently retired senior American Intelligence Officer published in that year his own observations on espionage. The officer, James MacCargar, chose the pseudonym Christopher Felix and called his *oeuvre The Spy and his Masters: A Short Course in the Secret War*. When this insider tackled the thorny question of 'sleepers', he observed:

A notable example of the 'sleeper' agent was the innkeeper whom the Germans introduced into the British naval base of

Scapa Flow not long after the First World War. He didn't stir during all the years until the outbreak of the Second World War; he was then able to provide the information which permitted a Nazi submarine to sneak into Scapa Flow early in the war, torpedo HMS *Royal Oak*, and escape untouched.[24]

With such widespread acceptance it is not surprising that in 1968 Cookridge returned to the subject in his biography of Kim Philby, *The Third Man*: 'It was clear that German naval intelligence had received detailed information about anchorage and defences, and that this was the work of a spy.'[25]

As we have seen, Wehring's existence had been discredited by McKee, but there was nevertheless a more widespread belief in an espionage angle to the loss of the *Royal Oak*. One theory centred on Prien himself, who, according to Geoffrey Cousins in *The Story of Scapa Flow*, had done his own reconnaissance work before the war:

Gunther Prien was the right kind of material for the special corps-elite of the German Navy, the U-boat fleet, and it was in pursuit of his dreams and ambitions that he spent a holiday in Orkney, apparently just a young tourist but, in reality, a spy.[26]

According to Cousins, Prien 'made a special study of the entrances to the flow and, realizing how well guarded and protected were the southern and western approaches, turned his attention to the easterly channel'. Since Prien had been killed in the North Atlantic, it was difficult for anyone to disprove (or substantiate) the claim. The idea certainly helped to resurrect the espionage role in the *Royal Oak* affair, even after so much imaginative talent had apparently gone to waste. The Home Office records show that no one bearing the more popular names of Wehring, Oertel or van Schullerman had either applied for or become a naturalized British subject. Even Orkney's Chief Librarian, David Tinch, who presides over Scotland's oldest public library (founded in 1683), has made a contribution to the spy's demise:

No watchmaker, Swiss or otherwise, worked in Orkney at that time, either on his own or in the employment of any of the local watchmakers. The name Albert Oertel is pure invention, probably derived from the name of the Albert Hotel in Kirkwall.[27]

The most complex theory of all was offered by Donald McCormick (using the pseudonym Richard Deacon) in his *The Silent War* in 1978. He acknowledged that Wehring had only existed in someone's imagination and advanced another idea based on an entry in U-47's log for 0120 hours on Sunday, 14 October 1939. Prien recorded in the log that he feared his mission had been discovered because the headlamps of a motor car travelling between St Mary and Kirkwall had momentarily focused on the U-47, which had then been negotiating the Kirk Sound on the surface. The Admiralty's Board of Enquiry agreed that Prien was unlikely to have fabricated such an incident for the press, but failed to trace the car driver. McCormick proposed an explanation for the reluctance of the driver to come forward:

. . . the mysterious driver proved as elusive as the fictitious Oertel: he has never been located. Is one possible explanation that the car driver was one of Canaris's under-cover agents whose job it was to frustrate Prien's mission? Bizarre as such a theory may seem, it is not impossible.[28]

The inescapable conclusion is that even if one disproves the existence of one spy (be he named Wehring or von Mueller, be he a watchmaker or an innkeeper), there will be plenty of commentators available to point out that the mere repudiation of one candidate does not eliminate espionage on the part of another.

Such speculation is untenable. In the years since the war considerable research has been undertaken to establish the exact circumstances of the loss of the *Royal Oak*. Wolfgang Frank and Alexander McKee, to name but two independent investigators, have spent many hundreds of hours examining every aspect of U-47's mission to Scapa Flow. They have been unable to find any evidence to support the idea that a German spy had played a part in it. Furthermore, Gerald Snyder, the author of *The Royal Oak Disaster*, actually traced all the fifteen living survivors of the U-47's original crew of forty-four. All denied the participation of any spy. One, Herbert Herrmann, who had been the youngest member of Prien's crew, has become a naturalized British subject and now lives in Dumfriesshire in Scotland. He is emphatic on the issue of Oertel, Wehring *et al*. and should be allowed the last word: 'This mythical German spy in the Orkneys simply never existed.'[29]

4

Who Was Werther?

There were about fifty agents attached to the network, each of whom supplied information on a particular field. Agents and sources were referred to in the messages to Moscow by their cover names, but contrary to the peacetime order, the identity of certain cover names remained unrevealed to one or the other of them, and sometimes to both. As a matter of fact, Rado's best agents remained 'unknowns' to the Director for a considerable time. 'Werther' reported on the German Army . . .

DAVID DALLIN in *Soviet Espionage*

The Swiss, of course, were aware that any day the same thing might happen to them that had happened to Denmark and Holland. Knowledge of Hitler's war plans was a matter of life and death for them. Rudolf Rössler delivered this information. From whom he got his information and how remains today one of the great mysteries of the annals of the secret services of the world.

MARGARET BOVERI in *Treason in the Twentieth Century*

There is only one credible source of the information – the British code-breaking centre at Bletchley Park in Buckinghamshire which, through the Counter-Intelligence operation codenamed 'Ultra', was in continuous receipt of Germany's war plans and intentions. Recently, I have secured confirmation of this from secret intelligence sources.

CHAPMAN PINCHER in *Their Trade is Treachery*

Shortly before midnight on 13 October 1943 a detachment of Swiss police surrounded a villa at 192 Route de Florissant, on the outskirts of Geneva, and made the final preparations for a raid that was to spark off the longest investigation into Soviet espionage ever known.

For the previous month the Swiss Bundespolizei (BUPO) had been monitoring transmissions from three different wireless sets, all apparently located in Switzerland. The first two, christened LA and LB, were based in Geneva. The third was thought to be in Lausanne. When BUPO's direction-finding equipment had positively identified the addresses from which the illicit signals were being broadcast, Inspector Charles Knecht of BUPO's Geneva office mounted the raid. The owners of the villa on the Route de Florissant were Edouard and Olga Hamel, two well-known communists whose radio shop in the rue de Carouge had been the subject of another police raid the previous year. On that occasion the police had been searching for subversive literature, and Hamel had been released from gaol after just two days. in custody.

While Knecht was searching the Hamel household a similar operation was being conducted at LB, the apartment of Margaret Bolli, at 8 rue Henri Mussard. Here the BUPO squad found a wireless transmitter concealed in a portable gramophone. By the end of the evening the Swiss police had seized two radios and four espionage suspects. The fourth person, Hans Peters, was Bolli's lover and turned out to be an Abwehr *agent provocateur*. He was subsequently released without charge.

BUPO's haul also included evidence of a considerable Soviet network operating in Switzerland and, indeed, further afield. On 20 November the set in Lausanne, known as LC, was confiscated, and its owner, an Englishman named Alexander Foote, arrested. LA, LB and LC became known inside BUPO as the 'Rote Drei' or Red Three.

From statements taken from the suspects and documents seized during the raids BUPO was able to reconstruct some of the traffic that had passed between the three illegal wireless stations and Moscow. BUPO was also able to identify the probable leader of the ring: a Hungarian Jew named Alexander Rado. Rado, who also lived in Geneva, promptly went into hiding and evaded arrest. Some of the captured cipher books enabled the Swiss cryptologists to put names to some of those mentioned in past wireless messages. Principal among these was a German refugee based in Lucerne, named Rudolf Roessler. He was eventually arrested by BUPO on 2 June 1944.

Roessler's arrest effectively eliminated what was left of the Soviet network in Switzerland, but a great many questions remained unanswered. Not surprisingly, the Swiss were anxious to discover why the Russians had taken so much trouble to finance and equip such a sophisticated and cosmopolitan organization on their territory. It soon transpired that Rado had been at the centre of an enormous network aimed at penetrating Nazi Germany. Before the fall of France, Switzerland had been used as a staging post for information passing between Berlin and Moscow. When the Soviet Embassy in Paris had been closed down Rado had been obliged to transmit his signals direct to Moscow. He had therefore been provided, initially at least, with three short-wave transmitters.

Two further questions remained to be answered: first, what was the quality of the information received from inside Nazi Germany, and second, who had sent it?

Evidence of the signals decrypted by the Swiss and the Germans during the war easily answered the first. The information received by Rado was excellent and had proved to be extremely reliable. For example, a signal on 29 April 1943 from DORA (an anagram of Rado) gave the Russians the exact timing of the German offensive on the Kursk salient, an advantage that tipped the balance against the attackers. The subsequent tank battle became a turning-point in the war. DORA's information could only have come from the top echelons of the Wehrmacht's High Command.

The precise answer to the second question, who had sent high-powered information from inside Germany through the LUCY ring in Switzerland for Soviet Russia, is what interests us here in this chapter. This particular section of the book is therefore less about a fact and its fables than about the hunt for the person, or persons, inside Germany who sent out material and around whose identity many myths have accreted. The answer is difficult to determine and can only be arrived at after a number of red herrings have been identified and discarded.

The identity of DORA's source became a matter of intense speculation, and it was soon established that his most significant intelligence dated from September 1942, the moment that Rudolf Roessler had been recruited into the Soviet network with the code-name LUCY. After his arrest Roessler acknowledged that he had indeed been the conduit for a tremendous quantity of information from inside Nazi Germany, but he consistently refused to name names. When the Swiss (and the Abwehr) succeeded in retrospectively decrypting LUCY's traffic, they learned that Moscow had shown the same inquisitiveness and had ordered DORA to ask LUCY for details concerning his sources. LUCY had steadfastly refused on security grounds, and Moscow had dropped the subject for fear of jeopardizing the flow.

Further analysis of LUCY's traffic revealed that a high proportion of his information was credited to just four people: WERTHER, TEDDY, OLGA and ANNA. As to exactly who these individuals were, no one could guess, although many tried. After the war the speculation

continued and the Allied counter-intelligence organizations tried to solve the puzzle. Much of the material
accumulated by the Nazis fell into American hands and
they continued the pursuit. According to a report written
by Wilhelm Flicke, the principal German cryptanalyst on
the case, some 5,500 messages passed between DORA
and Moscow during the three years the LUCY ring
operated. This extraordinary volume implied a total of
five transmissions per day, a truly remarkable achievement in wartime. Judging from the carbons found along
with the wireless sets, the Swiss reckoned on an average
monthly output of 140 messages. And of the 332 texts
acquired by the Americans, 137 specifically mentioned
WERTHER, TEDDY, OLGA or ANNA as sources.
DORA, of course, was receiving information from a very
wide variety of informants, but if the American sample
was anything to go by, some 42 per cent of the material
could be traced to LUCY's four mysterious sources. The
hunt was on. At stake were the identities of four heroes
(or traitors, depending upon your point of view) who
had been responsible for betraying a vast quantity of
strategically important Nazi information to Moscow.
Almost all the researchers and historians who took part
in the search for LUCY's sources were agreed on that
point, although there was considerable difference of
opinion on the speed with which the information reached
LUCY's radio stations. And the exact speed of delivery
might provide a clue as to source, for there would be few
people who would have been in a position to transmit so
much high-grade information so quickly.

The former chief of the German General Staff, Franz
Halder, went on the record to say in *Der Spiegel* on 16
January 1967: 'Almost every offensive operation of ours
was betrayed to the enemy even before it appeared on my
desk.' Allen Dulles, who wrote *The Craft of Intelligence* in

1963 after he had retired as America's Director of Central Intelligence, claimed: 'Roessler in Switzerland was able to get intelligence from the German High Command in Berlin on a continuous basis, often less than twenty-four hours after its daily decisions concerning the Eastern front were made.'[1] In all probability this appreciation of the time sequence was not Allen Dulles's own, although he had been based in Berne during the latter part of the war. It seems to have come from _Handbook for Spies_, written by Alexander Foote in 1949, in which he said that the Soviet network in which he had been a wireless operator had heard about decisions of Hitler's head-quarters 'within twenty-four hours' of them being made.

Foote's career had been far from ordinary. He was born in Liverpool and, when he left home, he went to work for a Manchester corn merchant. In 1935, aged thirty, he joined the Royal Air Force, but a little more than a year later he was given a discharge for failing to declare his membership of the Communist Party of Great Britain. Foote promptly decamped to Spain, where he joined the British battalion of the International Brigade. He stayed in Spain until September 1938, when he returned to London for formal recruitment by a Soviet agent. He was instructed to travel to Munich, where he remained briefly before taking up semi-permanent residence in Switzerland. There he worked for a Soviet network which operated independently of DORA's, but in the summer of 1940, after he had undergone a thorough wireless course, Foote was instructed to join forces with DORA and transmit messages under the code-name JIM. Foote's later career was subject to controversy and will be discussed further on in this chapter, but for the moment it is sufficient to say here that he did transmit messages for DORA and that Allen Dulles does seem to have taken the figure twenty-four hours from Foote's book and not from any CIA or other special source.

In a further account of *The Lucy Ring*, written by two French journalists, Pierre Accoce and Pierre Quet, the time lapse was further reduced to 'not more than ten hours' and 'in one instance it took less than six hours'. Which of these people is to be believed?

When the two Frenchmen published their book in 1967, it caused an uproar, for they claimed that Roessler had had a circle of ten intimate friends, all Bavarian Protestants, whose names 'are known to very few people'. Furthermore the journalists alleged that 'Rudolf Roessler first met his ten companions at the Front in the First World War and they became firm friends'. They were described as: 'Helmuth S, Hermann F, Rudolf G, Fritz T and Georg T, who were to become generals. O became a colonel and K a major. The last three, S, A and O, reached the rank of captain.'[2]

Having established LUCY's sources, the two Frenchmen explain how 'General Fritz T and Rudolf G, the "leaders" of the small conspiracy in Berlin'[3] were able to communicate with Roessler in Switzerland. Apparently:

General Fritz T had been able to get a small trunk through customs at Basle. It was a great risk of course, but it was the only way – time was running out. The trunk contained radio-telegraphic equipment: a short-wave transmitter-receiver, one of the latest models issued only to the Wehrmacht.[4]

Once the equipment had been smuggled into Switzerland Roessler was to ask a friend 'to assemble the set and teach him how to operate it. He would do the transmitting himself.' This arrangement suited everyone for

Fritz T agreed. He handed the equipment over to Roessler, with the codes and lists of wave-lengths that would be used.

Roessler's friends had meticulously laid their plans. Eight of them, simply by virtue of their posts, were at the very source of information concerning the Wehrmacht's movements. Each transmission of news concerning the army would be preceded by the word *Werther* – simply because the first two letters of Goethe's work are also those of the Wehrmacht. The other two conspirators, high-ranking officers in the Luftwaffe, would communicate any information concerning the air force, but it would pass through the same channel as the other. This news would be announced by a different signal, *Olga* – this being the name of Roessler's wife.[5]

This ingenious explanation was completed by the convenient fact that 'Fritz T was one of the assistants of General Fellgiebel, the head of the whole Communications Department'. This enabled the ten conspirators to transmit 'to Rudolf Roessler from the official broadcasting centre of the OKW [the Wehrmacht High Command]'.[6] Because Fritz T 'had practically the whole of the centre under his own control', he was able to send and receive messages from Switzerland without fear of discovery. This was made possible because

There were a number of wireless operators he could depend on – among them two sergeants, who had good reason to be grateful to him. Nothing ever surprised them and they never asked questions. In turn, they transmitted the messages of *Werther* and *Olga*, without knowing in the least what or to whom they were communicating.[7]

On the face of it this theory sounds plausible. The size of Roessler's circle was sufficiently large and well placed to provide LUCY's information, and the use of the OKW's own radio centre to transmit messages goes some way to explain the matter of communicating the intelligence. After all, the German direction-finding teams would hardly have monitored official channels and the sheer volume of the material precluded the use of couriers. However, Accoce and Quet also put other details in their book which were less plausible. For example, they identified the friend who was to teach Roessler how to use his transmitter as Christian Schneider. No sooner had this appeared in print in 1967 when Alexander Rado's own memoirs were published in Hungarian. In his book Rado said that Schneider knew nothing about radios. So who was right? If Accoce and Quet were wrong about Schneider, were their other details also erroneous?

Many expected Rado's book to solve the puzzles raised by other post-war observers. Foote had died in London in 1956, Roessler had died in December 1958, so Rado was the best qualified member of the network left alive who could end the speculations. In fact, he merely deepened the mysteries.

From his memoirs it is clear that Rado had managed to escape from Switzerland in September 1944 to report to the Soviet Embassy in Paris. He had been ordered to Moscow and, after a brief interlude in Cairo, when he considered remaining in the West under British protection, Rado had completed his journey and spent most of the following decade in Soviet labour camps. He had been released in 1955 and subsequently politically rehabilitated in Budapest, the capital of his native Hungary. His memoirs must have been published with the approval of the Party, and the political standpoint of the author is clear when, in his Foreword, he comments that 'reactionary circles refuse to this day to admit that they suffered military defeat as a result of the strategic superiority of the Soviet Union'.[8] Rado had evidently kept up to date with the continuing debate about the LUCY ring. He recalled that Marc Payot, who had headed BUPO's cryptanalysis team, had condemned Foote's *Handbook for Spies*, which, he alleged, 'positively teems with inaccuracies and even untruths'.[9] Rado had also noticed that two German historians, Wilhelm von Schramm and Gert Buchheit, had denounced Foote's book as well.[10]

Rado's motive in publishing his version, therefore, seems to have been a desire to correct Foote, and Accoce's and Quet's *The Lucy Ring*. He points out a number of errors common to both, among which was the suggestion that Roessler and Foote had been sending material to Moscow early in 1941, and that they had warned the Russians of the impending German attack. This was easily disproved by reference to the radio traffic itself, and the fact that 'Rudolf Roessler only became LUCY in November 1942 when we established contact with him on a regular basis.'[11]

Rado's account is important for two reasons. Firstly, he confirms that 'I never met Roessler myself – then or later.'[12] Then he testifies: 'I happen to know for a certainty that Schneider never worked as a radio operator and had not the vaguest notion of radio technology.'[13] Rado went on to say that: 'As for Roessler working independently with a transmitter of his own, people who knew him during that period say that he would not have known what to do with it.'[14]

On the question of the identity of WERTHER, Rado exploded the myth that Roessler had used the name to identify the Wehrmacht, rather than an individual person. 'The information Roessler passed on to us reached him from a variety of government departments in Germany. To help Central keep track of where the information came from I gave these sources suitable allusive codenames.'[15] Rado insisted that the 'statement that Werther was an invention of Roessler's is likewise without foundation'. According to his account: 'When I encoded the telegrams

I indicated the source with one of the above codenames, which were known only to the director and myself.'

In the face of mounting controversy about their version of events, Accoce and Quet admitted that they had made it all up. This was a satisfactory conclusion to Roessler's ring of ten friends, but it did not advance the case much in terms of establishing what really happened. Although Rado was understandably enraged by Accoce and Quet, he had to admit that 'on the subject of LUCY and his sources the record is a pretty tangled and distorted one'.[16] He confirms that in spite of Moscow's increasingly insistent demands to know the identities of LUCY's sources, 'he still flatly refused to give away their real names and ranks because, as he said, it could turn out to be disastrous for them. Appreciating this, we stopped pestering him with questions.'[17] Finally Rado is forced to conclude: 'There is every indication that LUCY's secret remains intact to this day.'

Rado's overall contribution to the debate was to confirm that he, not Roessler, had dreamed up the source-name WERTHER, but he failed to shed any light on the origins of the material.

Two further theories surfaced during investigations into *The Lucy Ring*. The first suggested that the Swiss Military Intelligence Service had operated a network in Germany throughout the war, and that Roessler had been fed this information because the Swiss were anxious to see Germany defeated. Such a ring did indeed exist, and it was code-named VIKING by the Swiss, who also maintained a link with Roessler via an officer named Hans Hausamann. When Hausamann was challenged on the subject during a television interview in May 1966, he acknowledged that he had received information from Roessler, and not vice versa. The possibility remains that Hausamann, who has since died in Switzerland, was under orders not to admit to having worked against the Germans. As a secret CIA report comments:

The fact is that certain Swiss officers were very directly a part of the activity of the Rote Drei. Understandably, this involvement remains a source of some concern to the Swiss, even today, because it is at odds with that strict neutrality which Switzerland has proclaimed for centuries as a buckler and breastplate.[18]

Soon after Hausamann's denial another of DORA's principal agents, a Swiss communist named Otto Pünter, published his war memoirs and alleged that General Alfred Jodl had been the source of the WERTHER material. So much of Pünter's information was so obviously inaccurate (like his assertion that LUCY was actually a source-name for information from inside the Reich air ministry) that it only complicated matters. The CIA later observed: 'Pünter's persistent muddying of the waters appears to serve Soviet purposes as well as his own.'[19]

The second theory to surface during investigations into *The Lucy Ring* was proposed by Malcolm Muggeridge in the *Observer* in January 1967 and was such as to make Pünter's efforts as a myth-maker pale into insignificance. Muggeridge suggested that Roessler had been working for the British, who had used him as a convenient route for passing ULTRA decrypts to the Russians. At first glance the idea seems fantastic, but there was a practical aspect to it. Christian Schneider, who had acted as a cut-out between DORA and LUCY, happened to be friendly with another member of DORA's organization named Rachel Dübendorfer, code-named SISSY. SISSY had also been a source of information for the British Secret Intelligence Service (SIS). Muggeridge's new theory had the British feeding Roessler ULTRA materials via SISSY.

In the absence of official statements on the subject from the traditionally silent British service, the idea gained currency.

The theory was fully established as a myth in 1980 by the publication of *Operation Lucy*, written by two television writers, Anthony Read and David Fisher. Their well-researched volume purported to explain exactly how the British had made Roessler a conduit to the Russians. They traced Alexander Foote's career and concluded that, before his recruitment by the Russians, Foote had volunteered his services as a double agent to the British and had been run as such by a senior SIS officer, Colonel (Sir) Claude Dansey. Since both Foote and Dansey were long since dead, the authors relied on circumstantial evidence to link Foote to SIS.

According to Read and Fisher, Foote was not the only member of DORA's network to be operating secretly for the British: 'Unknown to Rado, Rössler had also made contact with the British mission in Berne, where Count Vanden Heuvel was now installed as station chief of the Secret Service, answerable directly to Colonel Dansey in London.'[20] The effect of this was that 'the Soviet network in Switzerland' was 'virtually controlled by the British'[21] and, since 'its second-in-command and principal radio operator [was] a Dansey agent', the British decided to signal the contents of British decrypts direct to Foote, who, in turn, passed them on to Moscow.

This hypothesis is presented as fact by the authors, who inevitably fall back on the mystery surrounding LUCY's sources to justify what can be nothing more than conjecture. They assert that 'common sense alone denies the possibility of any single spy or group of spies, however highly placed in the OKW, where at most only thirty people, probably less, could have had access to the sort of information regularly received by Rössler'.[22] Their conclusion is reached by a process of elimination: '. . . there remains only one possible source for the most important material Rössler gave to Rado – the Ultra secret organization based in Hut 3 at the Government Code and Cypher School, Bletchley Park, Buckinghamshire, England'.[23]

This idea could probably be disproved by a comparison between DORA's radio traffic and the decrypts achieved by Bletchley, but such a time-consuming exercise is not necessary in this instance. The construction built by Read and Fisher depends on Foote's dual role as a British agent. This is simply untrue, and the authors themselves admit to some lack of comprehension concerning Foote's post-war treatment at the hands of the British Security Service, MI5.

At the end of the war Alexander Foote travelled to Moscow, where he underwent training for a new espionage mission to the West. However, in March 1947, Foote surrendered himself to an RAF patrol in Berlin and was interrogated by an MI5 officer, Michael Serpell, who flew over from London for the purpose. Foote claimed he had a change of heart politically and, after a month of debriefings in Germany, he was flown to London and installed in an MI5 safe-house. Here he gave a very detailed account of his wartime espionage, and it was Michael Serpell's report on the subject that became the basis of Foote's own autobiography, *Handbook for Spies*. Because Foote had not been privy to all of DORA's secrets his book contained innumerable inaccuracies. Indeed, Foote implied that LUCY's real identity was a Czech named Selzinger. When the second edition was released in 1964 Foote was dead and MI5 was disinclined to make the necessary corrections. The CIA's classified review of *Handbook for Spies* is sharply critical of the Security Service for promoting yet more falsehoods about the Soviet espionage network in Switzerland: 'Foote or his editors knew that the true name of Lucy was Rudolf Roessler. But instead of correcting the earlier errors, the 1964 edition compounded them by printing exactly what the French version had said except for the substitution of Roessler for Selzinger throughout.'[24]

The television writers Read and Fisher express surprise that Foote should have been subjected to an intensive MI5 interrogation.

One of the many intriguing questions about this whole episode is why Foote was held by MI5 at all. MI5 is the Security Service; MI6 is the Secret Intelligence Service. Granted that he was not one of that department's official agents, but since 1936 he had been working for them, albeit indirectly, via the Z Organization. Surely someone at MI6 must have known enough about his background and career to have spoken up for him?[25]

But the reason why SIS failed to intervene on behalf of Foote is perfectly simple: he had never been employed by them. Details of the alleged contact between Foote and Colonel Dansey are presented only in the vaguest terms by Read and Fisher, and their admission that SIS made no attempt to assist Foote after the war is itself proof that it owed him no debt of loyalty.

Both Foote and Dansey are now dead. So, too, are the others who are alleged to have been involved, such as Roessler and Vanden Heuvel. Nevertheless, there are two senior wartime SIS officers left alive who might have been expected to know about Foote's SIS role. One, Commander Kenneth Cohen, was Dansey's deputy. He is adamant that Foote had never been an MI6 agent. So, too, is Vanden Heuvel's chief assistant in Switzerland, Andrew King. Indeed, the idea that the British had manipulated the entire Soviet network in Switzerland has been described by Rado as 'the most fantastic hypothesis of all'.[26] Once again a plausible-sounding theory is found, on close analysis, to be built on very shaky foundations.

The same could not be said for Bernd Ruland's contribution in 1973, entitled *Moscow's Eyes*. In his book Ruland claimed that he had served as a communications officer at the OKW's radio centre at Zossen. There he had supervised a Wehrmacht major named Kemper and, in particular, two teleprinter operators who were part of an anti-Nazi conspiracy. Ruland claimed that he had developed some suspicions about their behaviour during the war, but it was only after the war that he had realized that the two young girls had supplied Kemper with the material that LUCY subsequently credited to WER-THER. Ruland obtained the consent of the two girls to document their experiences, on condition that he did not reveal their real names until after their deaths. On that basis Ruland was authorized to describe how the two women had purloined carbon copies of OKW teleprinter messages from *geheimschreiber* cipher machines. At some stage their supervising officer had challenged them, and he too had been drawn into the conspiracy. Ruland explained that he had made elaborate arrangements to protect the identities of the participants, including the two teleprinter operators who were referred to by the pseudonyms of von Parchim and Kalussy. Documents had been lodged with a Swiss bank, for eventual release to the Institute of Contemporary History in Munich. Unfortunately Bernd Ruland died on a train between Basel and Zurich soon after the publication of *Moscow's Eyes*. Neither his son, Dr Michael Ruland (a lawyer in West Berlin), nor his widow, Elisabeth Ruland, were able to shed any light on the matter. Nor, for that matter, could the chief archivist at the Munich Institute.

Interest in Ruland's book would probably have ended there if it had not been for a brief introduction to the

Hungarian edition, written in 1976, by Alexander Rado. In it Rado recommended the book because it 'deserves more attention than other books dealing with Soviet intelligence for the following reasons: The absolute reliability of the factual material presented, the accurate analysis of the events recorded, its anti-Fascist tone and the exciting nature of its contents [author's translation].' Rado went on to commend the book by assuring the reader that it 'provides answers to those so far unsolved riddles of how, and by what route, Soviet Intelligence acquired such large amounts of information from the highest levels of the communications centre of the Fascist German High Command'. He concludes by saying: 'I recommend with conviction this book to the reader. He is holding the kind of objective work in his hands which, in many ways, contributes to the general understanding, comprehension and evaluation of the secret war which was fought during World War II.'

This unique endorsement could only have been made with the approval of the Hungarian authorities and, perhaps because of this, some historians were quick to condemn Ruland. The Polish historian, Professor Garlinski, for one, described it as a 'classic tale of fiction', although in correspondence he has acknowledged that he has not actually read the book. He merely became aware of it some time after its publication. In any event, he says, 'the history is too simple, too much in the Hollywood style. If it had been possible to send top-secret information outside in this way, over some years, Hitler would have lost the war in a couple of months.'[27]

What then, is the solution to the conundrum? Was WERTHER really a pair of anti-Nazi teleprinter operators, or was LUCY's source altogether more sophisticated?

Professor Garlinski accepts that 'We are faced by a

puzzle which probably will only be solved by time . . .'.[28] Certainly one must agree with Rado that 'the contact between Lucy and his informants was ingeniously and expertly organized and worked perfectly'.[29] But according to recently released CIA documents, reproduced in *The Rote Kapelle*, there is a possible solution to the riddle of who was sending a vast amount of high-level Nazi information at speed to the LUCY ring for onward transmission to Moscow. A report previously classified as secret claims:

Despite the printed assertions to the contrary, Rudolf Roessler *did* divulge the identity of his sources, or at least some of them. Three and a half years before his death, he provided identifying information about four of his chief sources to a trusted friend. They were, said LUCY, (1) a German major – whom he did not name – who had been the chief of the Abwehr before Admiral Wilhelm Canaris assumed command; (2) Hans Bernd Gisevius; (3) Carl Goerdeler and (4) 'General Boelitz, deceased'.[30]

Although the CIA report neglects to identify the trusted friend, it is, in all probability the son of Xavier Schnieper, a Marxist and a journalist who, some twelve years younger than Roessler, had been instrumental in putting him in touch with Swiss Military Intelligence in 1940. Schnieper was one of Roessler's oldest friends and after the war was imprisoned in Switzerland (with Roessler) for spying for the Czechs. During an interview with Professor Garlinski in December 1979, Schnieper confirmed that Roessler had entrusted Schnieper's son with the secret of how, and from whom, LUCY had received his information. Twelve months after Roessler had died Schnieper's son was killed in a car accident. Evidently the CIA had somehow obtained an account of the conversation that passed between the two men.

There are, however, some remaining problems connected with the four candidates proposed by Roessler. The first person is easily identifiable, although Conrad Patzig was never a major. He was a naval captain and was replaced by Canaris in 1934. The second person was Hans Bernd Gisevius, a senior Abwehr official with a long history of opposition to Hitler. In February 1940 he was posted to Berne to act as a go-between for Canaris and his Polish confidante, Halina Szymanska. At the same time he was enrolled as a British agent and remained an important source for SIS until the 20 July plot, in which he participated and which he survived. That Gisevius supplied both the British and Americans with information is an established fact. But did he also give information to Roessler? He certainly knew Roessler and was also in touch with a German communist named George Blun, who ran his own Soviet network in Switzerland under the code-name LONG. The CIA note that 'Gisevius was sympathetic to the Soviet cause, a fact which became more apparent after the war than during it.'[31] It is also known that Gisevius was in the habit of using the Abwehr's daily courier from Berne to Berlin up to three times a week for his personal communications with Canaris's deputy, Hans Oster, and the other 20 July plotters. We can therefore assume that Gisevius had both the credentials and the means to supply Roessler. Roessler's third candidate was Carl Goerdeler, a former Major of Leipzig who resigned his post in 1936 as an anti-Nazi protest. Thereafter he was prevented from having any access to secrets, and it must therefore be assumed that Goerdeler's function (if any) was to act as a channel of communication to other conspirators. Like Canaris and Oster, Goerdeler was executed after the failure of the 20 July plot.

Roessler's fourth source, 'General Boelitz', is probably

Colonel Fritz Boetzel, head of the OKW's cipher department until 1939. He was later appointed to Athens to head the intelligence analysis branch of the German South-East Army Group. As such he had close links with the top levels of the Abwehr, and the CIA reported that he had been described by a subordinate as an anti-Nazi.

All of the people identified by Roessler as his sources appear to be plausible candidates. Unfortunately only Gisevius survived the war, and he is now dead. His autobiography, *To the Bitter End*, sheds no light on the subject and glosses over his role as a British agent between February 1940 and January 1945, when he successfully escaped from Berlin, posing as a Gestapo official. LUCY's radio traffic is equally unhelpful because on 19 May 1944 Roessler was arrested by BUPO and remained in custody until 6 September, when he was released on bail. In other words, during the vital weeks of the 20 July plot, LUCY was off the air.

The circumstances of Roessler's arrest, which followed that of Rachel Dübendorfer (SISSY) exactly a month earlier, confirms the existence of a link between DORA and the Swiss Military Intelligence Service. When BUPO investigators searched SISSY's home they discovered ninety-eight Swiss Intelligence documents concerning German troop movements. All were traced directly to a Captain Mayr von Baldegg, a Swiss intelligence officer based in Lucerne. This embarrassing turn of events, highlighting his connection with the Soviet network, resulted in a formal military tribunal, which heard the evidence against von Baldegg and promptly ordered his release and reinstatement. LUCY stayed in custody until September, but when his case was finally heard in October 1945 he was acquitted of espionage and the court acknowledged that he had rendered Switzerland a valuable service. The inescapable conclusion is that the Swiss at least were satisfied that LUCY had been working in their interests.

If all the reliable testimony as examined here is combined, and I believe Roessler and Rado to be reliable, it reveals a picture of DORA inventing the persona of WERTHER to act as a blanket cover identity for all LUCY's sources rather than as a name which refers to one individual informant. The same picture shows the ubiquitous Roessler juggling messages from several highly placed Abwehr officers. In all probability the officers used Gisevius as a conduit, although Dr Schnieper is reported as having mentioned the Abwehr's secure telephone cable between Berlin and Milan (with a courier from Milan) as a possibility. The CIA seems to agree: '. . . the characteristics of the LUCY messages and of their transmission from Germany to Switzerland suggest that Werther and the others probably had Abwehr communications channels at their disposal. There seems to be no plausible alternative theory.'[32]

Finally there is the mysterious group of anti-Nazis based at the OKW's radio communications centre at Zossen, described by Bernd Ruland and endorsed by Rado himself. If these teleprinter operators really existed (and the evidence is in their favour), might they not have been supplying the Swiss VIKING network as opposed to a Soviet network? The circumstances certainly appear to support such a theory. It would explain why the Soviets had no knowledge of the source. It would explain how the sources continued to provide top-grade intelligence at the very time that the Soviet-run rings were being rounded up by the Gestapo. Furthermore, if this information was being passed to Roessler on an official basis (in spite of Hausamann's diplomatic denials), it would explain the extraordinarily lenient treatment received by Roessler after his unfortunate arrest by BUPO. After so many years, and the death of so many of the important players, it is a certainty that the myths surrounding WERTHER will live on, but there is now enough evidence available to the serious researcher to discern the probable from the impossible.

5

Pearl Harbor: A Warning Ignored?

Intriguing pieces of evidence continue to surface that suggest that Washington knew – or ought to have known – of the impending attack in the mid-Pacific.

JOHN COSTELLO in *The Pacific War 1941–45*

To what extent, if any, did President Roosevelt have foreknowledge of the Japanese attack on Pearl Harbor in December 1941? Mythologists have been persistent in their claim that America's entry into the Second World War was the result of a sinister conspiracy in which Roosevelt and Winston Churchill played leading roles.

There can, of course, be no denying Churchill's jubilation at the news of America's decision to join the Allies against the Axis. He was absolutely delighted and his own announcement to the House of Commons of a declaration of war against Japan (at 3 P.M. on 8 December 1941) actually preceded the President's formal statement by two hours. The exact timetable took place as follows. The Japanese attack on Pearl Harbor began at 7.53 A.M. on Sunday, 7 December. In Washington it was lunchtime. Eighteen ships of the American Pacific Fleet were sunk or badly damaged, including eight battleships. One hundred and eighty-eight aircraft were destroyed (mostly on the ground) and 2,403 people were killed. Just after 4 the following afternoon (Washington time) Roosevelt signed a declaration of war against Japan, and had it passed by both Houses of Congress. Three days later, on the morning of 11 December, Hitler declared war on America. Congress reciprocated the next day.

From the Japanese point of view, the raid was a huge success. The Americans had clearly been unprepared, and a Commission of Enquiry under the chairmanship of a Supreme Court Justice, Owen J. Roberts, was promptly empanelled to establish whether army or navy personnel had been negligent. Even before the Commission had reached its findings the two principal commanders in Hawaii, General Walter Short and Admiral Husband Kimmel, were relieved of their commands, warned that they might face court-martial proceedings, and allowed to retire. But had they been negligent?

Neither man had been privy to the signals intelligence which had enabled certain senior officials in Washington to read Japanese diplomatic cable traffic and thus monitor the progress of the Japanese-American negotiations then current. In fact this useful source was the product of a secret Naval Intelligence operation code-named MAGIC, which had been decrypting Japanese machine ciphers, with varying degrees of success, since 1935. An important breakthrough in 1940 resulted in the American code-breakers solving the PURPLE machine cipher, the main Japanese diplomatic cipher. Those with access to MAGIC material correctly interpreted the warning signs contained in the telegrams passing between Tokyo and the Japanese ambassador in Washington. Thanks to these decrypts a general war alert had been distributed on 27 November 1941 and was in force at the time of the attack on Pearl Harbor, but General Short had concluded that the greatest danger to Hawaii lay in the threat of sabotage. He therefore concentrated all the aircraft under his command in large groups so they could be easily guarded. Unfortunately, his failure to disperse the planes made them ideal targets for the Japanese bombers.

Short and Kimmel took much of the blame for the tragedy, and in later years it became clear that they had made convenient scapegoats. Apart from the general war alert, neither officer had been told of the imminent collapse of Japanese diplomatic negotiations or the administration's conclusion that war was inevitable. Both battled to clear their name. General Short died in 1949, but Kimmel published his memoirs in 1955.

Although there was nothing in the PURPLE traffic to suggest that Pearl Harbor was a Japanese target, there were several messages in the lower priority J-19 code from the Japanese consul in Honolulu which betrayed an abnormal interest in Pearl Harbor and US shipping movements. J-19 was relatively easy to read but, owing to the volume of the MAGIC traffic, more decryption staff were devoted to the latter. It therefore took up to a fortnight for a J-19 despatch to be read, translated and distributed. In the aftermath of Pearl Harbor the J-19 decrypts were reviewed and found to contain a number of telling clues. On 24 September, for example, the Japanese consul in Hawaii was instructed to divide Pearl Harbor into five alphabetically coded areas and report all Fleet movements. His bi-weekly despatches were later turned into weekly reports, reflecting an escalation in Tokyo's interest in Hawaii. Evidently the intelligence analysts in Washington were too preoccupied to interpret these signs correctly.

The significance of the J-19 decrypts was only appreciated after the débâcle at Pearl Harbor. But was there other, firmer intelligence indicating an attack which reached the President but was later suppressed? Some historians believe this to be the case.

The controversy arose in 1972 when Sir John Masterman finally received British Cabinet approval to publish a document, *The Double Cross System in the War of 1939–1945*, which he had been commissioned to prepare in 1946 when still serving in the Security Service, MI5.

Masterman had retained an illicit copy of his wartime report and had arranged, through his OSS colleague Norman Holmes Pearson, to have Yale University Press publish it. The Security Service was appalled when it learned of his plan, but a combination of gentle arm-twisting by Masterman and some skilful negotiating by his solicitor, Christopher Harmer (himself a former MI5 case officer), succeeded in persuading Prime Minister Edward Heath to authorize publication.

Masterman's account of the Security Service's handling of double agents remains the definitive work on the subject, but it was his description of the man code-named TRICYCLE which revealed that in August 1941 the British had acquired information relevant to Pearl Harbor. Masterman and TRICYCLE play an important role in the events so it would be wise to expand here on the backgrounds of both.

Masterman was a distinguished Oxford academic who, in December 1940, had been invited to chair a special committee which had been set up to co-ordinate the information being passed to the enemy by a growing stable of British double agents. (This committee is sometimes referred to as the XX or Twenty Committee, and the system it controlled is sometimes called the Double Cross system.) MI5 had developed the necessary skills to run the double agents convincingly, but their continued performance required a steady flow of plausible high-calibre intelligence. Without a reasonable supply there was a danger of losing the Abwehr's interest, but there were considerable problems in judging exactly what pieces of genuine information should be delivered. Not everyone appreciated the possible opportunities and advantages offered by a comprehensive system of deception, so the agreed solution was a special committee which would consist of all the interested parties. In order to prevent the committee showing bias towards anyone, it was further agreed that Masterman would be a suitable candidate for the chairman and arbitrator. It is important to stress that the Security Service was already operating an impressive number of successful double agents long before Masterman took up his appointment and chaired the first Twenty Committee meeting on 2 January 1941. Several authors have erroneously credited Masterman with being the architect of the entire system. In fact that distinction belongs to Colonel T. A. Robertson, the MI5 officer who headed the section dealing with German double agents. Indeed, he had been running his first important German double agent before the outbreak of war. After the Twenty Committee had been wound up, in May 1945, Masterman wrote a review of its work for MI5's historical archives and returned to Oxford. Robertson, a career Security Service officer, remained in MI5. In the recollection of those who served in Robertson's section, Masterman never actually met a single double agent because there was no need for him to do so. He certainly never met TRICYCLE, and it will become clear that this is an important point.

TRICYCLE was originally an SIS agent, code-named SCOUT, who had volunteered his services to the British Secret Intelligence Service in Belgrade before the war. SCOUT, whose real name was Dusko Popov, then allowed himself to be recruited by the Abwehr and sent to spy in England. He reached London at the end of December 1940 and was passed by SIS into MI5's hands because, by bureaucratic convention, the Security Service retained responsibility for security and intelligence matters at home and within the Empire. SCOUT's journey to England had brought him into MI5's parish so his case came under its jurisdiction. Soon afterwards he received the Security Service code-name TRICYCLE. The code-name was chosen for him by his case officer, Ian Wilson, because he was to head a ring of three double agents: an MI5 nominee code-named BALLOON, the woman who became his lover, GELATINE, and his brother, DREADNOUGHT.

Following his apparent success in England, and after a couple of brief visits to Lisbon in January and March 1941, Popov received orders from his Abwehr controller to create a new spy ring in America. Arrangements for this mission were completed in mid-June 1941 and Popov set off on the first leg of his journey to Lisbon by flying-boat. He remained in the Portuguese capital until 10 August, when a place was secured for him on a clipper bound for New York via Bermuda. It is at this moment that the mythologists step into the story, for in Lisbon Popov was handed, by his German contact, a microdot containing a list of objectives for his new American network. The Abwehr's questionnaire is reproduced below, in full:

Naval Information – Reports on enemy shipments (material foodstuffs – combination of convoys, if possible with names of ships and speeds).

Assembly of troops for overseas transport in USA and Canada. Strength – number of ships – ports of assembly – reports on ship building (naval and merchant ships) – wharves (dockyards) – state and private owned wharves – new works – list of ships being built or resp. having been ordered – times of building.

Reports regarding USA strong points of all descriptions especially in Florida – organization of strong points for fast boats (E-boats) and their depot ships – coastal defence – organization districts.

Hawaii – Ammunition dumps and mine depots.
1. Details about naval ammunition and mine depot on the Isle of Kushua (Pearl Harbor). If possible sketch.

2. Naval ammunition depot Lualuelei. Exact position? Is there a railway line (junction)?

3. The total ammunition reserve of the army is supposed to be in the rock of the Crater Aliamanu. Position?

4. Is the Crater Punchbowl (Honolulu) being used as ammunition dump? If not, are there other military works?

Aerodromes

1. *Aerodrome Lukefield* – Details (sketch if possible) regarding the situation of the hangars (number?), workshops, bomb depots, and petrol depots. Are there underground petrol installations? – Exact position of the seaplane station? Occupation?

2. *Naval air arm strong point Kaneche* – Exact report regarding position, number of hangars, depots, and workshops (sketch). Occupation?

3. *Army aerodromes Wicham Field and Wheeler Field* – Exact position? Reports regarding number of hangars, depots and workshops. Underground installations? (Sketch.)

4. *Rodger's Airport* – In case of war, will this place be taken over by the army or the navy? What preparations have been made? Number of hangars? Are there landing possibilities for seaplanes?

5. *Airport of the Panamerican Airways* – Exact position? (If possible sketch.) Is this airport possibly identical with Rodger's Airport or a part thereof? (A wireless station of the Panamerican Airways is on the Peninsula Mohapuu.)

Naval Strong Point Pearl Harbor

1. Exact details and sketch about the situation of the state wharf, of the pier installations, workshops, petrol installations, situations of dry dock No. 1 and of the new dry dock which is being built.

2. Details about the submarine station (plan of situation). What land installations are in existence?

3. Where is the station for mine search formations [*Minensuchverbaende*]? How far has the dredger work progressed at the entrance and in the east and the south-east lock? Depths of water?

4. Number of anchorages [*Liegeplaetze*]?

5. Is there a floating dock in Pearl Harbor or is the transfer of such a dock to this place intended?

Special tasks – Reports about torpedo protection nets newly introduced in the British and USA navy. How far are they already in existence in the merchant and naval fleet? Use during voyage? Average speed reduction when in use. Details of construction and others.

1. Urgently required are exact details about the armoured strengths of American armoured cars, especially of the types which have lately been delivered from the USA to the Middle East. Also all other reports on armoured cars and the composition of armoured (tank) formations are of greatest interest.

2. Required are the Tables of Organization (TO) of the American infantry divisions and their individual units (infantry regiments, artillery 'Abteilung', and so forth) as well as of the American armoured divisions and their individual units (armoured tank regiments, reconnaissance section, and so forth). These TO are lists showing strength, which are published by the American War Department and are of a confidential nature.

3. How is the new light armoured car (tank)? Which type is going to be finally introduced? Weight? Armament? Armour?

1. Position of British participations and credits in USA in June 1940. What are England's payment obligations from orders since the coming into force of the Lend Lease Bill? What payments has England made to the USA since the outbreak of war for goods supplied, for establishment of works, for the production of war material, and for the building of new or for the enlargement of existing wharves?

2. Amount of state expenditure in the budget years 1939/40, 1940/41, 1941/42, 1942/43 altogether and in particular for the army and the rearmament.

3. Financing of the armament programme of the USA through taxes, loans and tax credit coupons. Participation of the Refico and the companies founded by it (Metal Reserve Corp., Rubber Reserve Corp., Defence Plant Corp., Defence Supplies Corp., Defence Housing Corp.) in the financing of the rearmament.

4. Increase of state debt and possibilities to cover this debt.

All reports on American air rearmament are of greatest importance. The answers to the following questions are of special urgency:

    I. How large is –
       (*a*) the total monthly production of aeroplanes?
       (*b*) the monthly production of bombers [*Kampfflugzeuge*]?

    (*c*) the monthly production of fighter planes?

    (*d*) the monthly production of training planes
        [*Schulflugzeuge*]?

    (*e*) the monthly production of civil aeroplanes
        [*Zivilflugzeuge*]?

  II. How many and which of these aeroplanes were supplied
to the British Empire, that is to say –

    (*a*) to Great Britain?

    (*b*) to Canada?

    (*c*) to Africa?

    (*d*) to the Near East?

    (*e*) to the Far East and Australia?

  III. How many USA pilots finish their training monthly?

  IV. How many USA pilots are entering the RAF?

Reports on Canadian Air Force are of great value.

All information about number and type (pattern) of front
aeroplanes [*Frontflugzeuge*]. Quantity, numbers and position of
the echelons [*Staffeln*] are of great interest. Of special importance is to get details about the current air training plan in
Canada, that is to say: place and capacity of individual schools
and if possible also their numbers. According to reports received
every type of school (beginners' – advanced – and observer
school) is numbered, beginning with 1.

The significance of the questionnaire lies in the fact
that it undoubtedly reveals a strong German interest in
Pearl Harbor. A copy of Popov's microdot objectives was
made by the local SIS Station in Lisbon and communicated to London, where it was translated in time for it to
be read to the Twenty Committee at its regular, weekly
meeting on Tuesday, 19 August 1941.

By the time the Twenty Committee had absorbed the
document, Popov had arrived in New York and had been
introduced to the FBI by his SIS contact, John Pepper.
Pepper, who headed the Secret Intelligence division of
British Security co-ordination in New York, had escorted
Popov on the final leg of his journey and was on hand to
introduce the Yugoslav to his link with the Bureau,
Special Agent Charles Lehrman.

After the publication of Masterman's book in 1972 these events were recounted, with a greater or lesser degree of accuracy, by Popov himself in *Spy Counter Spy*. Popov's mission to the United States as TRICYCLE was not entirely successful and he returned to England, via Lisbon, in October the following year. In the meantime the Japanese attacked Pearl Harbor, and Masterman commented:

TRICYCLE was to operate in the United States generally and would presumably be for some length of time in the eastern states. It is therefore surely a fair deduction that the questionnaire indicated very clearly that in the event of the United States being at war, Pearl Harbor would be the first point to be attacked, and that plans for this attack had reached an advanced state by August 1941.

Obviously it was for the Americans to make their appreciation and to draw their deductions from the questionnaire rather than for us to do so. Nonetheless, with our fuller knowledge of the case and of the man, we ought to have stressed its importance more than we did.[1]

This observation by Masterman led to a host of myths and was seized on by Popov in his own book, where he elaborated on this apparent failure on the part of MI5 to emphasize TRICYCLE's reliability. Masterman went on to say in *The Double Cross System*:

With the greater experience of a few more years' work, we should have risked a snub and pointed out to our friends in the United States what the significance of the document might be; but in 1941 we were still a little chary of expressing opinions and a little mistrustful of our own judgement. The lesson is, no doubt, that once an agent is firmly established, any questionnaire given to him has a much greater and more immediate intelligence value than that usually attributed to it.[2]

Popov interpreted these remarks as meaning that the FBI had failed to spot the significance of that part of the questionnaire relating to Pearl Harbor, and that in Masterman's opinion correct appreciation of the questionnaire might have averted the Pearl Harbor disaster. Is this view justified?

What Popov did not know was that, even though MI5 accepted him as a double agent, he was always the subject of discreet surveillance. The flat provided for him in Mayfair by the Security Service had been wired for sound, and the flat above was permanently manned by MI5 personnel. Although Popov, and perhaps Masterman, believed that his acceptance had been complete in December 1940, this was far from the case. MI5 had not been prepared to give him a complete bill of health, and this may have coloured the FBI's view of him. Certainly the Bureau was exceedingly wary of him, and MI5's reluctance to vouch for its agent would have undermined his standing.

As we have already seen, Popov received his questionnaire shortly before catching his plane for Bermuda on 10 August 1941, and presented the SIS Station in Lisbon with a copy. His account of this, published thirty-three years later, is somewhat inaccurate. For example, Popov says that he left London for Portugal on 22 June 1941,[3] while Masterman's document puts the date four days later.[4] This is relatively unimportant, but his version of receiving the questionnaire was later to acquire an unexpected significance. Popov recalls a meeting with his Abwehr controller, whom he knew as Ludovico von Karsthoff, and reading the questionnaire for the first time: 'The first paragraph was headed "Naval Information". I glanced at the second paragraph. It concerned the assembly of troops for overseas transport from the US and Canada . . .'[5]

It was only after Popov had had a glass of champagne that he returned to examine the questionnaire further:

Picking up the list of questions I glanced at it while still sipping my second glass of champagne. This time I read further: The second heading was Hawaii. The Tirpizufer was asking for information about ammunition dumps and mine depots on the Isle of Oahu, where Pearl Harbor is located.[6]

Popov claims in 1974 that he immediately concluded in 1941 'This was the Japanese target':

I communicated the news of the impending attack on Pearl Harbor to Lisbon poste-haste. They got on to London, and I was instructed to carry my information personally to the United States, since I was leaving in a few days. Apparently, they thought it preferable that I be the bearer of the tidings, since the Americans might want to question me at length to extract the last piece of juice.[7]

The mythmakers made short work of this account. The chief mythmaker in this instance is Pulitzer prize winner John Toland, described by the publishers of *Infamy* as 'America's foremost historian of the World Wars'. In writing *Infamy* Toland's central theme was that 'Roosevelt and the inner circle had known about the attack'.[8] Because there is no reference to the attack in the MAGIC decrypts before 7 December 1941, Toland presumes Popov's information must have been the source. Toland suggests that Popov 'had personally passed on to the FBI a detailed plan of the Japanese air raid which he had obtained from the Germans'.[9]

Somehow Popov's questionnaire had been transformed by Toland into 'a detailed plan', which had apparently been communicated to the President, who then deliberately suppressed it.

The incident described by Popov in which the Abwehr's questionnaire was handed over appears differently in Toland:

He was asked to study a questionnaire. The second heading startled him. It was Hawaii. He was to locate ammunition dumps and air-fields on the island of Oahu and learn complete details of Pearl Harbor, including pier installations, number of anchorages and depth of water.[10]

Toland then reproduces 'the British Secret Service translation of the complete German questionnaire'. It is, however, not complete. In fact the original (see above) has been edited to exaggerate its relevance to Hawaii. Toland has omitted the entire first paragraph, thus leaving the document with the title 'Hawaii'. His 'complete' questionnaire ends after the second sentence of the Special Tasks section: '*Special tasks* – Reports about torpedo protection nets newly introduced in the British and USA navy. How far are they already in existence in the merchant and naval fleet?'

By omitting the next 400 words, which form twelve further sections with ten sub-sections, Toland leaves the reader with the impression that the Abwehr's questionnaire is exclusively concerned with Hawaii and, in particular, with static torpedo nets. In reality, the reference to the nets is in the context of ships at sea. As a result, Toland's version of the questionnaire is misleading. Not surprisingly considering the magnitude of the disaster at Pearl Harbor, hindsight has encouraged both Popov and Toland to stress the Hawaiian sections. But how was the questionnaire as a whole seen in context at the time by others?

Most myths are exceedingly difficult to run to earth, especially with the passage of time, but in this particular instance many of the participants survived the war and were able to record their version of events. Take, for example, the visit made by Popov to the SIS Station in Lisbon soon after he had received the Abwehr questionnaire. Under normal circumstances further investigation would have been made impossible by the secrecy surrounding that organization. Yet, fortuitously, the SIS officer in charge of British espionage in Portugal during 1941 is alive and living in the United States, beyond the jurisdiction of the Official Secrets Act. Commander Philip Johns RN has the distinction (though it is not regarded as that by SIS) of being the only wartime SIS Head of Station ever to have published his memoirs. He recalled, in *Within Two Cloaks*, that Popov's

arrival was reported to me and the fact that he had been given by his German controllers a questionnaire relating to the US defences of Pearl Harbor. At the time, if I remember correctly, little importance was attached to this piece of information, and if of value it would have been for the Americans to assess, although at that time the USA had not entered the war.[11]

Clearly the SIS Head of Station, who was an experienced intelligence officer, running one of SIS's most important outposts in a neutral capital, did not discern an impending Japanese air raid on Pearl Harbor. If he had failed to grasp the significance of Popov's questionnaire, was Masterman entirely justified in his assertion that the questionnaire 'indicated very clearly' that 'Pearl Harbor would be the first point to be attacked'? With the advantage of hindsight, the rhetorical question seems a little contrived, but in the circumstances prevailing at the time neither the FBI nor MI5 would have been justified in lecturing the Americans on the implications of the questionnaire. It should be remembered that at the time Popov had not yet proved his *bona fides* to the Security Service. He was, after all, primarily SIS's agent, and that organization had not enjoyed particularly impressive experiences with Continental agents. The majority of MI6's European networks had collapsed during the summer of 1940 following skilful German penetration.

Both Ian Wilson and Bill Luke, Popov's first two MI5 case officers, have confirmed their initial caution about their agent, who is remembered as a likeable rogue. Certainly Popov's post-war career (and, indeed, that of his brother, Ivo, code-named DREADNOUGHT) was chequered by various brushes with the police of several different countries that more than justified MI5's circumspection. It is difficult to imagine the youthful members of the Twenty Committee pinning their reputations on an agent with such doubtful credentials. So how, then, was Popov received by the Americans?

According to Popov, he had to wait weeks before he was granted an audience with J. Edgar Hoover, and when it finally took place it lasted less than thirty seconds. On his own admission he clashed with the FBI Director on the subjects of morals, espionage and corruption. His information was dismissed as being 'too precise, too complete to be believed'.[12] Furthermore, Hoover prohibited the Yugoslav from travelling to Hawaii to undertake his mission for the Abwehr. Hoover wrote an amusing account of his meeting with Popov, without identifying him by name, in the *Reader's Digest* of April 1946 entitled 'The Enemy's Masterpiece of Espionage':

One day in August 1941 we met a youngish traveler from the Balkans on his arrival in the United States. We knew he was the playboy son of a millionaire. There was reason to believe he was a German agent. With meticulous care we examined his possessions, from toothbrush to shoes. While a laboratory agent was holding an envelope so that the light slanted obliquely across its surface, he saw a sudden tiny gleam. A dot had reflected the light.

After this coup the FBI apparently found the German agent anxious to co-operate:

Under questioning the Balkan playboy was bland and affable. Seeing that we knew about the dots, he began to talk freely. He had studied under the famous Professor Zapp, inventor of the micro-dot process, at the Technical High School in Dresden.

Hoover seems to be taking the credit for intercepting a genuine enemy spy: he does not mention that he was told of his arrival by MI5. Nevertheless, the article illustrates the point that Hoover believed he was dealing with an enemy agent as opposed to a trusted British informant. A decade later Don Whitehead returned to the subject in *The FBI Story*:

Then a young Balkan arrived in New York City from South America. He checked into his hotel and didn't appear surprised when he found two FBI agents waiting for him in his room. There was no reason for surprise, because, even though recruited by the Germans as an espionage agent, it can now be revealed that he was working for the FBI.[13]

This dramatized version seems closer to the truth than Hoover's, in that Popov is correctly described as a double agent, but there is no mention of the information relating to Pearl Harbor. Instead the Balkan's microdot is said to have

opened a door through which the FBI got on to the trail of espionage agents and their confederates, a trail that led through the United States and South America, and helped the FBI break up a German espionage ring in Mexico in co-operation with the Mexican Government.

This, of course, is the purest fantasy since Popov's job had been to set up a new network (not join an existing one), and Hoover had prevented him from even starting his mission. Popov was eventually obliged to return to England, where he embarked on the third, most successful phase of his espionage career, as a double agent operating for MI5. It was in the light of this final episode in Popov's relationship with MI5 that he really proved his worth, and that Masterman was tempted to speculate on the implications of the Abwehr's questionnaire.

So is there any further evidence to suggest that Roosevelt was ever informed of Popov's alleged warnings? Toland himself admits that Hoover's second-in-command, Edward Tamm, had never heard of the questionnaire,[14] but adds, somewhat disingenuously, that in Tamm's opinion, 'if Hoover had received such information . . . he would certainly have passed it on to Roosevelt'. Hardly conclusive proof, or even circumstantial evidence, suggesting that Hoover had ever discussed Popov's case with the President.

There was a curious sequel to Popov's story in August 1982 when he died at his home in Opio, in the South of France. Two eminent historians, Ronald Lewin and H. Montgomery Hyde, wrote to *The Times* pointing out various aspects of Popov's extraordinary wartime exploits. Montgomery Hyde suggested that 'each copy of the questionnaire, amounting to some 15,000 [*sic*] words, was accommodated within the compass of a single microdot'.[15] Montgomery Hyde concluded, in the best traditions of a wartime myth:

In my view, Dusko Popov's disclosure to us of the microdot considerably outweighed his failure, through no fault of his own, to convince the FBI of the truth of Japanese plans in Hawaii, which the FBI's chief, J. Edgar Hoover, chose to ignore, thinking that Popov's information about the impending attack on Pearl Harbor was false.

It is now clear that, through the J-19 decrypts, the Americans were aware of a perceptible escalation of Japanese interest in Hawaii in late 1941 and also that Japanese-American diplomatic relations were at near breaking-point. But it is hindsight to suggest that the questionnaire handed by the Abwehr to one of MI5's double agents offered definite foreknowledge of a Japanese attack. Even the sections relevant to Pearl Harbor can hardly be described as a blueprint for an attack. At the time no one noticed the significance of the information, and no one handed it on to President Roosevelt or Winston Churchill.

But was there anyway a conspiracy between Roosevelt and Churchill to draw the United States into what was, in 1941, essentially a European conflict? John Toland believes so, and the extraordinary case of Tyler Kent has been cited as evidence that, long before the Axis had threatened American interests, the President had engaged in secret talks with Churchill with a view to the creation of an anti-Nazi alliance.

The story of Tyler Kent began in October 1939 when the twenty-eight-year-old diplomat was transferred from his post at the American Embassy in Moscow to cipher duties at Joseph Kennedy's Embassy in London. Kent, who professed to be strongly anti-Semitic, was soon involved in right-wing politics in London, and in particular with a semi-secret group known as The Right Club. The Right Club had a total membership of about two dozen, and was led by a Unionist Member of Parliament, Captain Archibald Ramsay. He and his wife, an equally vociferous opponent of the Jews, held regular meetings at a White Russian tea-room in South Kensington. Also in attendance at these meetings were several MI5 informants, who kept the Security Service well briefed on The Right Club's activities. Significantly, these agents reported to a case officer in the counter-espionage division, rather than someone from the branch dealing with political subversion.

Kent seems to have been kept under fairly constant

X-BEAM ANTENNAE

The *X-Gerät* radio aerial similar to those located at Calais and Cherbourg which, on the afternoon of MOONLIGHT SONATA, transmitted a series of navigational beams to guide the Luftwaffe to its targets. Before the bombers took off on their mission two test signals were routinely made, a procedure which allowed the RAF to calculate the path of the beams and identify the enemy's targets

Mata Hari's Netherlands passport, issued by the Dutch Consul General in Frankfurt-am-Main in August 1914. Her status as a neutral enabled her to travel throughout wartime Europe, but the Spanish entry and exit stamps on her passport show that she was only in Madrid for forty-eight hours at the time she was alleged to have been conducting a lengthy affair with William Canaris

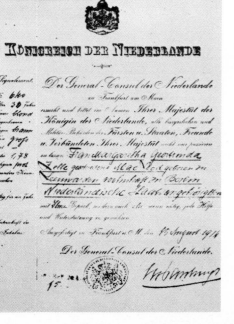

KONIGREICH DER NIEDERLANDE

The French identity card forged by MI6 for Halina Szymanska, the Polish intermediary between Admiral Canaris and the British Secret Intelligence Service. The fictitious details on the card describe her as 'Marie Clenat', and enabled her to meet the Abwehr Chief in German-occupied territory. The revelation of her secret role ended years of speculation concerning the Admiral's true loyalties

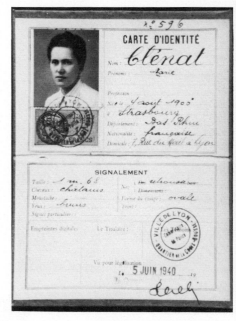

HMS *Royal Oak,* the battleship which blew up and sank with the loss of 833 lives in the supposedly impregnable Scapa Flow. The Admiralty eventually established that the disaster had been caused by U-boat attack and not sabotage as had first been suspected, but how had a submarine managed to penetrate the heavily defended anchorage? One popular explanation identified a German spy based in Kirkwall who had masterminded the operation and then made his escape back to Germany

The victorious U-47 returns to Kiel on 23 October 1939 and is saluted by the crew of the German cruiser *Emden*. Wartime and post-war accounts of the night attack on HMS *Royal Oak* differed on so many points that some historians believed the submarine's log had been altered to conceal the involvement of a German spy

Bernd Ruland, a warrant officer in the communications centre of the Wehrmacht High Command in Berlin's Bendlerstrasse. In June 1941 he discovered two of his teleprinter operators were stealing carbon copies of top-secret orders and handing them to a contact for delivery to a Swiss-run spy ring. Instead of turning in 'Angelika von Parchim' and 'Maria Kalussy', he joined their network and protected them after the war. Significantly, the Hungarian edition of Ruland's book carried an authenticating foreword by Alexander Rado, wartime head of the LUCY ring

A rare photograph of three teleprinter operators at the German High Command's secret communications centre. The *geheimschreiber* ('secret writer') was a ten-rotor ciphering teleprinter which boasted much greater security than the more widely used, manually operated, Enigma machine. Messages were printed automatically onto paper tape, which was then cut up and pasted onto military telegram forms. According to Bernd Ruland, two operators were able to remove a roll of duplicate tape and smuggle it out of the building for onward transmission to Switzerland

A *geheimschreiber* operator preparing a message for automatic transmission along teleprinter lines. More than 120 specially selected female operators lived in the 'Lager Duppel' at Zehlendorff in the south of Berlin and travelled in to work on the S-Bahn. These girls operated a bank of twelve teleprinters inside a 'secret room' and were responsible for the encryption of the Reich's most sensitive operational orders

Alexander Foote, the British-born wireless operator who ran one of the LUCY ring's three illegal Soviet radios in Switzerland. The speed with which he acquired top-secret information from Germany and transmitted it to Moscow led to speculation after the war that he had also worked for the British Secret Intelligence Service, channelling ULTRA intelligence from GCHQ at Bletchley to the Russians. In fact, as he admitted to his Security Service debriefer in August 1947, he had no idea where the LUCY ring had obtained its information. His autobiography, *Handbook for Spies,* was written by an MI5 officer, Michael Serpell, but is now regarded by the CIA as a work of disinformation

Alexander (Sander) Rado, the Hungarian leader of the LUCY ring in wartime Switzerland who operated under the anagramatic code-name DORA. Recruited in Moscow in 1924, Rado married Lenin's secretary and, from 1936, directed a Soviet spy network from his home in Geneva until September 1943. He escaped arrest by fleeing to Paris the following year and ended up in Moscow, where he was imprisoned for treason. He was released in 1955 and was politically rehabilitated by the Communist authorities in Budapest. He published his memoirs in 1976, but failed to end the controversy surrounding his network's chief source of information

Rudolf Roessler, the LUCY ring's key figure and, reputedly, the only person to know the real identity of WERTHER, the code-name given to the network's main source. Born in Germany, Roessler took political refuge in Lucerne in 1933 and was later recruited by Swiss military intelligence. He played an ambiguous role in the Soviet ring, but always refused to divulge his sources of information. He died in December 1958, apparently taking his secret to the grave. However, according to a secret report on wartime Soviet espionage prepared by the CIA, Roessler did confide in a trusted friend three years before his death

Dusko Popov, the Yugoslav double agent who was instructed by his German controllers in August 1941 to travel to the United States and build a spy ring. Popov's mission failed because the FBI was unwilling to co-operate, and Popov returned to London where he continued to deceive the Germans until May 1944. After the Japanese attack on Pearl Harbor in December 1941 the Security Service realized the full significance of an Abwehr questionnaire Popov had been provided with before embarking on his mission to America. Writing after the war, FBI Director J Edgar Hoover claimed the credit for identifying Popov as a dangerous Nazi spy

Commander Philip Johns, the British Secret Intelligence Service Head of Station in Lisbon who received a copy of Dusko Popov's Abwehr questionnaire. It contained a list of tasks which he was to undertake, and some of it related to the defences around Pearl Harbor. Some historians later suggested that the text of the document obviously heralded an airborne attack on Honolulu, but John insisted that 'little importance had been attached to this piece of information'

The German Kommandantur at Enverneu, headquarters of the German 302nd Infantry Division, commanded by Major-General Conrad Haase. Among the documents recovered by Allied intelligence officers from this building during Operation JUBILEE was an order placing the Dieppe garrison on alert. Nevertheless, the warning was unspecific and demonstrated convincingly that although an attack had been expected along the French and Belgian coasts, the Wehrmacht had little idea of the exact target

Ludwig Moyzisch, the former Sicherheitsdienst chief in wartime Ankara who ran the spy code-named CICERO between October 1943 and April 1944. In 1950 Moyzisch, who had retired to Innsbruck, published *Operation Cicero* and revealed that the British Ambassador's valet had, at the height of the war, routinely photographed the contents of the safe at the British Ambassador's residence. Embarrassing questions were asked in the House of Commons and Sir Hughe Knatchbull-Hugessen, the retired Ambassador, declined to confirm or deny the story. Twelve years later CICERO himself emerged to give a fuller account of his remarkable espionage

Elyesa Bazna, one-time valet to the British Ambassador in Ankara and Nazi spy extraordinary. Bazna was not identified by name when the story of Operation CICERO was first revealed in 1959, but he eventually collaborated in the writing of his auto-biography *I Was Cicero*. After the war Bazna had been imprisoned for passing counterfeit notes. The Sicherheitsdienst had paid for his espionage with forged British currency. Bazna wanted to sue the German government for compensation and believed the book would finance the litigation. His case was quickly thrown out of court. Some historians now believe he had deceived the Germans by working as a double agent for the British

Colonel Monty Chidson, the seasoned British Secret Intelligence Service officer whose mysterious presence at the British Embassy in Ankara led to speculation that he had secretly run CICERO as a double agent. In fact, Chidson had suffered a nervous breakdown in England and had been posted to Turkey as a sinecure. His unsuccessful investigation into a leak at the Embassy caused Elyesa Bazna to hand in his notice and escape capture

'All British agents were volunteers. Each was thoroughly investigated, interviewed many times to determine psychological and intellectual motivation and fitness, and, if finally accepted, subjected to a rigorous course of training. Here MADELEINE is practicing "blind drops", parachuting from a moving aircraft at night. The figure behind her is the jump master.' This photograph, which appeared with the above caption in *A Man Called Intrepid,* was credited to 'the BSC Papers, Station M Archives'. In fact, it is a movie still from a feature film made at Pinewood Studios after the war. The thriller, entitled *School for Danger,* starred Jacqueline Nearne and Harry Ree who both appear in this miscaptioned photo

surveillance until the moment of his arrest on 20 May 1940. When Special Branch detectives, accompanied by an MI5 officer, raided his flat in Gloucester Place, they recovered copies of more than 1,500 telegrams, all purloined from the Embassy's code-room. Many of the telegrams were communications that had passed between the then First Lord of the Admiralty, Winston Churchill, and President Roosevelt. Ambassador Kennedy had already withdrawn Kent's diplomatic immunity so the raid, and his arrest, could take place.

Although these details did not become known immediately, the Home Office did release a public statement on 2 June 1940 concerning Kent's arrest. *The Times* carried this report under the heading 'American Detained by Home Secretary: Former Employee at US Embassy':

In consequence of action taken by the American Ambassador, in co-operation with the British authorities, Tyler Kent, a clerk who has been dismissed from the employment of the American Government, has been under observation, and has been detained by order of the Home Secretary.

Kent was charged with offences under the Larceny Act and the Official Secrets Act and was sent for trial at the Old Bailey. He was convicted at the end of October and sentence was postponed until 7 November, when the trial of a fellow member of The Right Club, Anna Wolkoff, was concluded. Kent was sentenced to seven years' imprisonment for theft and breaches of the Official Secrets Act by Mr Justice Tucker. Although the two trials had been held *in camera*, newspaper reporters were admitted into the court to hear the Judge sentencing. The following day *The Times* reported the case under the heading: 'Secrets Case Ended: Seven Years for Embassy Clerk'.

Kent served his term in Parkhurst Prison on the Isle of

U.W.-E

Wight and was eventually deported home. The leader of
The Right Club, Captain Ramsay, who had been shown a
selection of stolen telegrams by Kent, was never convicted
of any offence but was detained under the Emergency
Regulations. His detention received considerable publicity and widespread coverage was given to the consti-
tutional question raised by the imprisonment of one
Member of Parliament on the order of another.

Yet according to Toland, anxious to promote the
Roosevelt-Churchill conspiracy, news of these events was
suppressed by the British authorities. He explained that
'in England all trials under the Official Secrets Act were
held *in camera*'.[16]

In fact Official Secrets Act trials were, and are, relatively unusual events, and there were only four during
the entire course of the war, including those of Kent
and Wolkoff. (The others were Douglas Springhall and
Ormond Uren.) All were reported by the press, although
it is true to say that reporters were generally excluded
while sensitive evidence was being heard. Toland ignored
the many newspaper stories and maintained:

> It was not until June of 1944 that the news of Kent's
> imprisonment was released by chance. It came after a Member
> of Parliament asked a question about Captain Ramsay [*sic*],
> who had been imprisoned without charge the last four years. It
> was then revealed that Kent had given him some of the secret
> Roosevelt-Churchill messages. An American reporter filed this
> story, which surprisingly passed the British censor.[17]

But, as we have seen, the story of Kent's conviction
and imprisonment was made public in *The Times* and
other papers at the time of the Central Criminal Court
trial in 1940. Much of the actual proceedings were held *in
camera*, but this alone cannot constitute evidence of a top-
level political conspiracy. It has long been a convention in

England that evidence from members of the Security Service, MI5, be heard in closed court. Responsibility for prosecuting the case against Kent and Wolkoff was in the hands of the Solicitor-General, Sir William Jowitt, a Labour Member of Parliament since 1922 and therefore Churchill's political adversary. Certainly Jowitt himself had felt no qualms about participating in the Kent-Wolkoff case. It is evident from Jowitt's *Some Were Spies*, which was the first detailed post-war account of the events that had taken place in the Old Bailey in November 1940, that he had no reservations about the case. Indeed, his book contains his impressions of eleven other important prosecutions. It would have been easy for the author to have omitted the two chapters that deal with Kent and Wolkoff, but Jowitt did not choose that course. If a conspiracy existed between Roosevelt and Churchill, Jowitt seems to have been a most unlikely fellow-conspirator.

In terms of evidence the basis of the allegation against the President and the Prime Minister seems to be founded on the flawed arguments that Dusko Popov had warned the administration of an air raid on Pearl Harbor, and that Tyler Kent's imprisonment had been a matter of political expediency. Analysis shows that neither case holds water.

6

Jubilee or Betrayal?

To the writing of books about Operation Jubilee, the raid by the 2 Canadian Division on Dieppe in August, 1942, there appears to be no end. One book on the subject has already been published this year; here are two more.

GORONWY REES, reviewing *Dieppe: August 19* and
Dieppe: The Shame and the Glory in 1963

Lord Louis Mountbatten had planned a commando raid on to French soil for the end of June 1942. The idea was to land, gather intelligence, alarm the enemy, divert attention from the hard-pressed Russian front and then to withdraw. Code-named Operation RUTTER, it was postponed because of bad weather. Cancelled altogether on 7 July, it was then reinstated as Operation JUBILEE and scheduled for 18 August. Known to us as the Dieppe raid, it was a disaster. Had the Germans known about the raid beforehand?

Late in the evening of 18 August 1942 a force of 237 ships slipped their moorings in the Solent and made a course for the French coast, sixty-seven miles away. Operation JUBILEE was under way and it was, depending upon whose public announcement you listened to, a 'commando raid' or, as Churchill later described it, a 'reconnaissance in force'. The target was the port of Dieppe, and the Allies had deployed more than 6,000 troops to execute the plan. By midday on 19 August the force had been decimated on the beaches and had suffered 3,623 casualties. Hardest hit was the Canadian contingent, which comprised three-fifths of the troops taking part in the amphibious landing: of 4,963 Canadians involved, only 2,210 returned to England safely. Their losses of 907 killed and 1,840 taken prisoner amounted to a terrifying 68 per cent rate of attrition. Every one of the forty-six tanks taken across the Channel was lost.

In the weeks following the carnage at Dieppe any number of reasons were put forward to explain what had gone wrong. Some said the overall plan had simply been too ambitious. The idea had been to make a frontal assault on the town's beaches, having eliminated the coastal artillery placed on top of the two headlands on either side of the main attack area. Once the town had been cleared of the enemy, a perimeter was to have been established on the outskirts and defended while specialist teams undertook various intelligence missions in the captured buildings. Once these had been completed the five-mile perimeter was to have been reduced and an orderly withdrawal staged. To ensure complete surprise the initial assault was to have been made without the benefit of a naval bombardment or air attack.

In the event the operation quickly collapsed into a shambles. The two major German defensive positions proved impossible to silence, and the troops and tanks landed on the beach were cut down in a murderous crossfire. When the battle-weary survivors limped back to England the Chief of Combined Operations, Lord Louis Mountbatten, hastily called together a conference of all concerned. The post-mortem took place in London on 20 August, and all those invited were given an opportunity to express their views on what had gone wrong. One Canadian officer suggested that the Germans 'had possessed foreknowledge of the operation . . .'[7] Mountbatten cut him off with a curt warning that as he was satisfied no breach of security had occurred he would hear no further comments of this nature.'[1] Nevertheless, the speculation continued.

The 'point of no return' for the raiders was scheduled for 0300 on the morning of 19 August. The force reached that point, some ten miles from its target, on time and continued the channel crossing. But at 0130 two British radar stations, at Newhaven and Beachy Head, had reported spotting a small force of enemy ships converging on the JUBILEE fleet. Two warnings were transmitted to the command vessel, HMS *Calpe*, but neither was received. Forty-seven minutes past the point of no return eight German ships suddenly found themselves in the path of what they perceived as an invasion fleet. Five of the vessels were small coastal steamers and they promptly headed for the safety of the shore. The three escorts, all fast motor gunboats, engaged the fleet and then withdrew, badly damaged. Although the British had no way of knowing it, the senior German officer in command of the convoy, First-Lieutenant Wurmbach, had failed to alert the coastal defences because his wireless aerial had been shot away in the first few moments of the engagement.[2] Nevertheless, star shells had been fired and the JUBILEE force had every reason to believe that they had lost the element of surprise. Those on the raiding party who had seen the star shells and the gunboats presumed the Germans on shore had been primed. Confirmation that Wurmbach's frantic warning had failed to get through did not come until later in the day, until the commandos stormed a German strongpoint at Varengeville, some four miles to the west of Dieppe.

Several documents were seized during the fighting, including a guardbook which logged incoming orders. One entry, dated 10 August, had come from Major-General Conrad Haase, commander of the two battalions of the 571 Infantry Regiment assigned to garrison Dieppe.

The first part of his orders stated: 'The information in our hands makes it clear that the Anglo-Americans will be forced, in spite of themselves, by the wretched predicament of the Russians to undertake some operation in the West in the near future.'[3] The Germans had, therefore, been in a state of general overall readiness for more than a week before JUBILEE was launched, and off-duty gun crews had been required to sleep fully clothed. In fact the commandos discovered that these orders had been ignored by some German troops, who were found undressed in their quarters. The guardbook also revealed that Haase had only raised the invasion alarm at 0500, more than an hour after Wurmbach's first contact with the invaders. These guardbook entries suggest that, although the Germans were generally alert to the possibility of something happening in their area in 'the near future', they were not expecting anything that particular night. They had no detailed foreknowledge. So where did the idea originate, and how did it gain credence?

The Canadian officer who raised the matter with Mountbatten was not alone in thinking that he had led his men into a trap. A secret survey conducted by the postal censor in the weeks following JUBILEE revealed that 5 per cent of Canadian survivors writing home blamed their heavy casualties on a betrayal. But Terence Robertson notes: 'The sense of betrayal shared by this minority had nothing to support it.'[4]

The controversy was fired after the war by reports from returning prisoners of war that the Germans had actually boasted of having been forewarned. Colonel Robert Labatt of the Royal Hamilton Light Infantry recalled being interrogated by a German intelligence officer who explained that he had been kicking his heels in Paris waiting for the raid to take place. Was this the truth, or was it merely an attempt to demoralize a prisoner?

The idea that the Germans had obtained some warning of the raid was, therefore, a matter of concern in the months following JUBILEE. The suspicion that a well-placed spy had succeeded in penetrating the operation's tight security gained further credence after the war through the works of three authors: Stanley Lovell, Gunter Peis and Leonard Mosley. All suggested that an enemy agent had managed to pass the word. Were these authors right? What were their sources?

In January 1941 the Security Service relinquished control of the information handled by their growing stable of double agents to the Twenty Committee. Most of the double agents were authentic Abwehr spies who had changed their loyalty or undergone a 'turning' process. Handled by a conscientious MI5 case officer, each fed their German controllers with a specially prepared diet of damaging misinformation combined with a plausible quantity of genuine information. Maintaining the correct balance was a difficult, not to say fraught, skill, and individual case officers were understandably anxious to acquire details of likely-sounding plans to retain the enemy's interest. In 1963, what amounted to doubts concerning the Twenty Committee's handling of JUBILEE were articulated.

In that year Stanley Lovell, a former Director of the American Office of Strategic Service's Research and Development Branch, published his wartime memoirs *Of Spies and Stratagems*. In them he related a number of stories about what 'he saw, heard and did' whilst serving in OSS. In Chapter 15 he dealt with the Dieppe raid and suggested that the British Secret Intelligence Service had accidentally tipped off the Germans. It had apparently happened when the raid had been postponed unexpectedly. Instead of transmitting the information too late for the Germans to take action, SIS had let a double agent send a message to the Abwehr more than twenty-four hours before the troops landed on the beaches. According to Lovell:

At the appointed time the little invasion fleet made its rendezvous off the English coast in the fog. The SIS, we can be sure, knew all about it. After an agreed upon waiting period, the German radio operator was given a message to flash to Berlin. 'A great Commando raid is laid on, destination Dieppe. Biggest operation since Dunkirk evacuation. Scheduled for Dieppe. Time: Tuesday at dawn.'

Lovell suggests that the German double agent had been used in a similar way during the raid on St Nazaire three months earlier. The spy had sent 'accurate but retarded information' after the success of the operation had been assured. On this occasion the same spy was to repeat the exercise: 'The message was to be sent late Monday evening and this would be another accurate but "just too late" bit of intelligence.'[5]

The hitch in the plan concerned Mountbatten's alleged failure 'to arrive and to sail on Sunday night'. This caused the operation to be delayed by twenty-four hours but strict radio silence had prevented anyone from informing SIS: 'So Sunday and all day Monday, Broadway (SIS) had no way to receive news of the delay and naturally proceeded on the timetable they had been given. Late Monday evening the message went over the air to Berlin.' Lovell concluded: 'The dangerous game of maintaining a supposed London spy ring information service to the Germans had by mischance and a delay at a rendezvous caused the death of perhaps 2,000 brave Commandos.'[6]

This remarkable account is obviously in error in two respects: Lord Louis Mountbatten did not accompany the raiders (nor did he ever intend to) and the raid actually took place on Wednesday, 19 August. However, neither detail is particularly relevant to the main thrust of the crucial allegation, which, if true, provided the Germans with rather more than thirty-six hours' warning of the attack.

These two inaccuracies are counter-balanced by two items which suggest that Lovell knew more than is apparent at first reading: he was himself in a position of considerable authority as Director of OSS's Research and Development unit and, as OSS's principal scientist, had been privy to many of the important technical advances. He might well have had access to privileged information concerning JUBILEE, especially when one considers that American troops had also taken part in the operation. The second point in his favour is his reference to a ring of double agents in London controlled by SIS. The fact that MI5 and SIS had indeed run a stable of double agents remained a closely guarded secret for a further nine years, until the publication in 1971 of Farago's *Game of the Foxes* and Masterman's *The Double Cross System* the following year. So if Lovell had been indoctrinated into the existence of the double agents, it is conceivable that he might have known about the information they were transmitting at the time of Dieppe.

In his book, Masterman singled out the Dieppe raid as an example of an operation that had been launched without the benefit of a cover plan or a deceptive contribution from MI5's double agents; he categorically states: 'It is sad, but interesting, to speculate whether the Dieppe raid might not have been more successful, or at least less costly, if it had been effectively covered.'[7] Masterman's opinion is not to be dismissed lightly on this occasion, for he was the Twenty Committee's chairman and, therefore, the officer responsible for co-ordinating the material being prepared for the enemy's consumption.

By 1977 the German author Gunter Peis claimed, in

his book *The Mirror of Deception*, to have discovered new evidence which

seemed to prove that the Germans had, paradoxically, been forewarned of the raid by the British themselves. In the case of Dieppe this would mean that Churchill had knowingly, though not lightly, delivered up five thousand men, mostly Canadians, to the German bayonets waiting for them.[8]

During the course of his research Peis had traced 'double agents, intermediaries, radio operators and officers at the German end of the secret "London sources" who were still able to confirm the fatal advance warning of the attack on Dieppe'.[9] Several different interviewees apparently confirmed that 'on 13 August 1942 a "very reliable, proven agent" who was living in Southern England reported to the Abwehr on an impending landing at Dieppe'. Two former Abwehr officials are quoted directly:

'In mid-August 1942,' the former head of the Hamburg Abwehr station, Kapitan zur See Herbert Wichmann, told me, 'a radio agent in England told us about preparations for a landing in the Fécamp area. Fécamp is only about fifty kilometres west of Dieppe.'

This recollection was reinforced by Oberleutnant Wein, who 'recalled that a further advance warning reached the Germans through another direct radio contact from England to Hamburg-Wohldorf: "In 1942 thirty-seven-two-five also warned us about a landing operation that was to take place near Dieppe." '[10]

The reference to 3725 is of special interest because the German agent known to the Abwehr by this code-number was also known to MI5 under the code-name TATE. If TATE really had alerted his controllers in Hamburg, he could only have done so with MI5's assistance and

approval. Peis also identifies three other possible
warnings:

The former agent-controller of the Lisbon station, Herr von
Carnap, confirmed that during one of their meetings in Lisbon
Ostro had reported to him about an impending landing near
Dieppe.
The former chief of counter-espionage of the Abwehr,
Oberstleutnant Hans Freund, told me that the Abwehr had
received yet another warning about Dieppe from a Croat agent
in Istanbul.
The final and most unambiguous advance warning about a
'landing at Dieppe in the immediate future' came from Istanbul.
Here the agent was E800, whom the British were using as a
double agent.

Thus, according to Peis, the Abwehr received warnings
from TATE, OSTRO, a Croat and E800, no less than
four separate agents, of whom two were operating under
British control. This led Peis to comment: 'Dieppe – so it
now seems – was the deception operation *par excellence*!'

Perhaps prompted by Peis's research another author,
Leonard Mosley, wrote *The Druid* in 1981 about 'the spy
who double-crossed the double cross system'. Mosley was
described by his publishers as having

uncovered evidence that one man escaped the English net – a
man called the Druid. Following up on rumours he heard as
long ago as 1942, Mosley has sifted through old dossiers and
tracked down sources in Britain, Germany and elsewhere to
piece together the astonishing story.

Mosley himself wrote in his own book that the Allied
raid on Dieppe was unambiguous: 'It was quite obvious
from the start that the Wehrmacht knew they were
coming, and had made all the necessary preparations. It
was the Druid's first success.'[11]

Mosley suggested that the Druid was the code-name

given to the German spy who had landed in England on the night of 10 May 1941 and had roamed free, undetected by the British authorities. Dieppe, said Mosley, 'was one of the costliest disasters of the war, and the Druid helped to make it so'.[12] With Mosley's contribution, the Dieppe myth gained further credence. Whereas Lovell and Peis agreed that warning of JUBILEE had been a communications failure initiated by the British, albeit with the best of intentions, Leonard Mosley suggested the existence of an entirely unknown spy. Was this likely? Did the Druid really exist?

Mosley suggests that the Druid parachuted into Wales on the same night as another German agent named Karel Richter, on 10 May 1941, and that on landing the Druid made contact with Arthur Owens, who was living in the Swansea area. However, Richter parachuted into England on 14 May 1941 and Arthur Owens was actually residing at HM Prison Dartmoor at the time, where he had been since March 1941.

But perhaps variations in date and domicile are insufficient to create doubt about the authenticity of Mosley's Druid. Maybe it would be worth examining some of Mosley's ideas in detail.

Mosley suggests that while he was trying to find out more about the Druid he had uncovered a number of Soviet moles in British Intelligence: 'Indications of the identity of some of these individuals will be found in the narrative which follows.'[13] Although Mosley admitted to 'recreating some of the incidents, reconstructing and rejigging others', the author confirmed that

all the code-names (both Nazi and SIS) used in this narrative are the actual ones by which the agents involved were known during World War II. So are all the names of the characters – with four exceptions and I have concealed their identity for personal reasons.[14]

Mosley explains that 'on the night of May 10, 1941'

the first spy, a seasoned Abwehr veteran named Captain Heinz Richter, landed in the flat marshlands of Lincolnshire, in eastern England, and was immediately taken into custody by the British security police. He had £4,000 in British sterling in his money belt and a supply of explosives and dried secret ink.[15]

But the facts, which are publicly available both at the Lord Chancellor's Office and at the Public Record Office in London, are as follows: Richter was not the first spy; by 14 May 1941 (the real date of his arrival) no less than nine German agents had been arrested in England and of this number three had already been tried, convicted and executed. Karel Richard Richter held no military rank and was far from being 'a seasoned Abwehr veteran'. In reality he was a marine engineer on the Hamburg-Amerika liner SS *Hansa* who had fled to Sweden from his native Czechoslovakia in November 1939. He had been deported to Germany in July 1940 and had been recruited by the Abwehr the following November. He parachuted into a field near London Colney (in Hertfordshire) early on the morning of 14 May and was taken into custody by Police Constable Alec Scott of the Hertfordshire Constabulary at approximately 11 P.M. the following night. He was found to be carrying $1,000 and £300 Sterling.

Mosley then goes on to refer to MI5 as 'the internal wing of SIS',[16] whereas MI5, the British Security Service, is the organization responsible for intelligence and security in the United Kingdom and in all other British territories. It is separate from SIS, the Secret Intelligence Service, which is known as MI6. Then in his account of the Dieppe raid Kim Philby is described as 'the liaison officer between MI5 and MI6, the two principal branches of the SIS',[17] whereas at this time Philby had not even joined MI6. He did not do so until September 1941. Philby was never a member of MI5.

Mosley then goes on to identify an Abwehr agent, code-named ARABEL by the Germans and GARBO by the British, as Luis Calvo. In July 1980 I traced Luis Calvo to Santander in Spain and interviewed him. He denied having operated as a double agent for the British and helped to identify GARBO for me. I later spoke to GARBO and received his version of events. They were unquestionably two different people.

Finally Mosley reconstructs the Druid's discovery of JUBILEE's target (Dieppe) and presents Kim Philby and Tommy Harris, a case officer in MI5's Spanish Section, at a meeting of the famous Twenty Committee chaired by Colonel T. A. Robertson, at which Colonel Robertson apologized for failing to provide a cover plan for the Dieppe operation. At that time Robertson did indeed head the MI5's B1(a) Section responsible for the running of German double agents. I asked Colonel Robertson personally if such a meeting had ever taken place. He denied it.

I then talked to other retired MI5 case officers who had been responsible for running double agents back to the Abwehr. All were particularly incensed by Mosley's suggestion that 'as became known later, at least two and probably four MI5 officers working within the Double Cross System and manipulating captured Abwehr agents were also working for the KGB'.[18]

Not surprisingly, this allegation outraged the B1(a) survivors, who described the book in a joint letter to the *Daily Telegraph* on 5 January 1982 as a 'deplorable slur' and threatened to take legal action to prevent the British publishers, Eyre Methuen, from labelling *The Druid* as non-fiction. Sadly the Security Service declined to allow anyone access to long-defunct files for evidence. MI5 refused to be dragged into a public court battle, even if the reputation of its former officers was at stake.

The only remaining mystery concerning *The Druid* is Mosley's sources. The name of a former SIS officer mentioned in the text and quoted in the introduction as having helped the author is Rodney Dennys, but Dennys denies ever having discussed the matter with Mosley.

In an interview on the BBC *Newsnight* programme on 5 January 1982, Mosley named Kim Philby as another SIS officer who had helped him in his research. This seems unlikely, bearing in mind that details in *The Druid* concerning Philby are wrong. Nor is Philby the most reliable of witnesses. Under detailed examination Mosley's narrative betrays too many mistakes for the non-fiction label to be justified. Therefore I doubt the existence of the Druid, as does Colonel Robertson and all the other members of B1(a) that I have contacted. In the light of the above, it seems even more improbable that such a person provided the Germans with advance warning of the raid on Dieppe.

And what about other spies and double agents? Might they not have participated in the Dieppe disaster? The Abwehr's own records state that an agent identified by the number A3924 informed them of a possible raid in the Dieppe sector on 4 August. Although A3924's exact identity remains uncertain, there is a strong likelihood that it was OSTRO, an Abwehr agent based in Lisbon who made a lucrative living from peddling items of intelligence. His German case officer believed him to be in control of a substantial network of informants in England. In reality OSTRO was Paul Fidrmuc, a Sudeten Czech who manufactured his information from gossip, guesswork and a small collection of pre-war reference books. Not only did OSTRO identify Dieppe as a probable target (without the benefit of privileged sources), but later in the war he was correctly to predict an Allied assault on Normandy. OSTRO's forecasts proved so accurate that at one moment SIS attempted to trace him so that he could be placed under control or eliminated. Surprisingly, Fidrmuc survived the war and died in Portugal in 1958.

Let us now return for a moment to one of the first people to suggest that SIS had accidentally tipped off the Germans, Stanley Lovell, former director of OSS, author of *Of Spies and Stratagems* and, as I explained before, a man privy to much high-level information.

If A3924 informed the Abwehr, it cannot have been TATE because we know he was number A3725. However, it looks as though Lovell did think it might have been TATE who sent the accidental signal because Lovell says of the double agent: 'The surrender of Germany ended the usefulness of the German radio operator – but not the promise of Britain.'[19] This hint narrows the field considerably, for the only one of the double agents who operated a wireless set in 1942 and continued to transmit right up until May 1945 was TATE, who worked on through the last days of the war, and enjoys the thanks (and protection) of the British Security Service up to the present day. TATE, who now lives alone in a modest semi-detached house an hour's drive from London, is extremely sensitive about the charge made against him by Lovell but is understandably reluctant to enter a public debate on the subject. Nevertheless, he is emphatic that no such signal was ever sent over his transmitter. His memory on the issue is supported by the radio technician most intimately associated with his case, Russell Lee, who has also denied any participation in JUBILEE. He should know, for TATE was never permitted to key his own messages.

Could the message have been about RUTTER and not

JUBILEE? Did someone decide to capitalize on an abandoned plan by feeding details of RUTTER to the enemy through a double agent, only to be caught by the reinstatement of JUBILEE? For, it must be remembered, the original plan, code-named RUTTER and scheduled for the end of June 1942, had been postponed, then cancelled on 7 July and then reinstated as JUBILEE on 18 August. The reinstatement of a cancelled operation was unusual because it was so insecure. One realizes the risks involved when one considers the reasons for RUTTER's cancellation. They were 'the continuing bad weather and a German Air Force attack on two assault ships which, loaded with troops, lay ready to sail for Dieppe at Yarmouth Roads'.[20]

Clearly there was an opportunity for advantage here, but TATE, his Radio Security Service supervisor, Russell Lee, and TATE's MI5 case officers have denied any involvement. Critics might say 'well they would, wouldn't they', but there is corroboration to be found elsewhere. Masterman is quite specific that no cross-channel deception plans were authorized at this time. MI5 had proposed using DRAGONFLY, a Briton of German descent named Hans George who had operated as one of MI5's double agents since January 1941. It had been suggested that he cover the activities of the amphibious forces in the Solent, but the idea had been turned down, as Masterman says:

In May Lord Swinton had proposed that there should be discussions with Lord Louis Mountbatten about the possibility of using our agents in connection with the Isle of Wight. It was suggested that DRAGONFLY, if moved to the neighbourhood, could give the Germans sufficient information to prevent them from creating new sources of information there, and that the operations of the CCO from the island could thus be effectively covered. This plan did not mature for reasons that were by then only too familiar . . .[21]

The conclusion to be drawn from these denials is that no double agent in Britain sent a tragically timed signal. But what about from elsewhere? Perhaps from Istanbul?

Security for the Dieppe operation was so extraordinarily tight that it was decided even not to let the three Service intelligence organizations into the secret.

The exclusions of other staffs is presumably explained by the concern for secrecy; this certainly became a first consideration once RUTTER had been cancelled. Knowledge that the operation had been revived as JUBILEE was confined to the Prime Minister, the Chiefs of Staff and the staffs immediately involved.[22]

Indeed, not even the organization responsible for the preservation of secrecy, the Inter-Services Security Board, was informed about JUBILEE until after the operation had been completed!

It therefore seems unlikely that the Druid, TATE, OSTRO, J. C. Masterman or anyone in MI5 were implicated in a Dieppe raid conspiracy. So what actually happened?

On 23 June 1941 a Luftwaffe reconnaissance flight had succeeded in photographing concentrations of landing craft and other invasion vessels along the south coast of England, particularly in Newhaven and Cowes.

On 20 July the Joint Intelligence Committee in London had completed a comprehensive review of the level of German readiness along the French and Belgian coasts and had concluded that the enemy was not yet expecting the Allies to make major landings.

On 4 August the Abwehr suspected that there would be some future enemy operations in the Dieppe sector but did not know what to expect, nor when, nor exactly where. In all probability this general unease about future enemy action contributed to Major-General Haase's decision of 10 August to have his troops sleep fully clothed. German documents captured at Dieppe at the time of the raid make it clear that, although Haase had ordered his garrison into a state of readiness on 10 August, they had not been placed on alert until 0500 hours on the morning of the raid itself. An analysis of the Wehrmacht's records by Professor Campbell of McMaster University has also established that if the Abwehr did possess advance warning, they certainly failed to pass it on to Field Marshal von Rundstedt's headquarters.

The complete lack of any telegrams to von Rundstedt about an impending attack suggests that the Wehrmacht had no foreknowledge: documents further support the proposition that no prior warning was given. But might this be interpreted as indicating that the Abwehr had simply neglected to mention the impending attack to von Rundstedt's staff? If such a lapse had happened there would probably have been a major investigation afterwards, but there is no trace of any such incident.

What however remains clear is that the German cryptographic service had succeeded in breaking some of the Royal Navy's low-grade ciphers, thus enabling them to monitor the unmistakeable build-up of British shipping in the Solent. The Germans had also noticed the strict radio silence before the operation began and recognized that this was a change in the pattern of routine signals. The Germans also intercepted BBC broadcasts warning the French civilian population in the occupied coastal zones about future Allied operations. Naturally these messages were very general in nature and certainly did not specify the timing of planned offensives, but they were enough to alert the Germans. But despite these snippets of intelligence the Wehrmacht had no definite foreknowledge of the actual target. The German alert extended along the entire French Channel coast, and no special emphasis was placed on Dieppe. Moreover, as Professor Hinsley's official history of *British Intelligence in the Second World War* concluded: 'As may be judged from the slow response of the German Air Force, the raid achieved tactical as well as strategic surprise.'[23]

In this chapter the various stories surrounding the disastrous raid on Dieppe in 1942 have been examined. At the time of the débâcle, which cost so many Allied lives, many people believed there had been a leakage of information to the Germans. Doubt was cast on JUBILEE's claimed watertight security. Yet the Abwehr's records, and even details from the guardbooks kept by Dieppe's German garrison, support the view that there was no breach in the operation's secrecy.

There was, of course, plenty of intelligence available to the Germans to enable them to foresee a major landing on the French Channel coast; inadequate Allied signals procedure should have been enough to send the occupiers into a full-scale alert, but von Rundstedt's headquarters were caught unprepared. Although, superficially at least, the Twenty Committee's double agents make plausible-sounding scapegoats for JUBILEE's failure, there is no evidence to support an allegation of treachery or ineptitude.

7
Cicero: A Stratagem of Deception?

Originally, I believed that Cicero must have been a British 'plant'. My short 'cloak and dagger' existence having been spent in 'A' Force and with MI5 and MI6 officers of the calibre of Michael Ionides, I did not believe in a British ineptitude that would permit someone like Bazna actually to spy on us successfully. In the light of events which took place in England, now I am not so sure.

DAVID MURE in *Master of Deception*

On 18 October 1950 the British Foreign Secretary, Ernest Bevin, made a remarkable admission concerning the wartime conduct of Sir Hughe Knatchbull-Hugessen, Britain's ambassador to Turkey between 1940 and 1945. His poor security had led to the loss of several extremely sensitive documents to the Germans.

The story of the spy known as CICERO is well documented. He had been employed by Sir Hughe as his valet, and he had also been employed by the Germans to photograph the contents of the ambassador's dispatch box and personal safe. The affair was made public in 1950 by Ludwig Moyzisch in his book *Operation Cicero*. The author claimed to have been the Sicherheitsdienst's representative in Ankara during the war and had been responsible for running CICERO as an agent between October 1943 and March 1944. Moyzisch's account was substantiated by the former German ambassador to Turkey, Franz von Papen, although neither revealed CICERO's real name. The book caused a sensation and not a little discomfort to Sir Hughe, who had by then retired from the Diplomatic Service to his country home in Kent. Evidently Moyzisch's publisher in London, Allan Wingate, was more than slightly concerned about his author's reliability because he added an unusual note:

Operation Cicero, as here related, is as accurate as at present can be ascertained but is written from the German standpoint and presents the German side of the affair. Relevant Allied documents may eventually be released which, no doubt, will complete the story. We have no hesitation in publishing the manuscript as it stands for its excitement, readability, and historical interest.

Moyzisch's tale was followed by a feature film entitled *Five Fingers*, starring James Mason, but it was not until 1962 that CICERO himself surfaced, in Munich, and collaborated with a German author to write *I Was Cicero*. CICERO turned out to have been an Albanian named Elyesa Bazna, whose chief motive in declaring himself seems to have been a desire to extract a pension from the German government. Moyzisch had paid CICERO for his information in forged British currency to the face value of £300,000, which had resulted in Bazna serving a prison sentence in Turkey for passing counterfeit notes. Bazna felt that he was entitled to some compensation, although the German government rejected all his claims.

The story would probably have remained there, a true account of wartime espionage, if further disclosures had not undermined it.

The first contribution came, in 1963, from Allen Dulles. His brief comment on CICERO in *The Craft of Intelligence* cast doubt on the value of the information passed by Bazna: 'Contrary to the general impression, there is no evidence that the Nazis gained from Cicero any information about the planned invasion of Europe except possibly the code word for the operation – "Overlord".'[1] He also pointed out a fact highlighted by Moyzisch but ignored by Bazna: 'In the Cicero case. Ribbentrop and the diplomatic service suspected deception.'

Three years later Dulles revealed his own personal involvement in the CICERO case in *The Secret Surrender*, an account of the events which led to the surrender of the Nazi forces in Italy in April 1945. Dulles had been the OSS's chief representative in Switzerland during the latter part of the war (from November 1942) and one of his agents, Fritz Kolbe, had supplied him with German Foreign Office documents describing CICERO's activities. Kolbe (whom Dulles only referred to by the code-name GEORGE WOOD) had started supplying Dulles with copies of German telegrams in August 1943. The second batch was delivered on 7 October 1943. During the following sixteen months GEORGE WOOD made three further visits to Dulles in Berne and, by the end of the war, had produced 1,600 classified documents. Dulles commented:

Of direct practical value of the very highest kind among Wood's contributions was a copy of a cable in which the German Ambassador in Turkey, von Papen, proudly reported to Berlin (in November, 1943) the acquisition of top-secret documents from the British Embassy in Ankara through 'an important German agent'.

Dulles realized the gravity of the leak and

immediately passed word of this to my British colleagues, and a couple of British security inspectors immediately went over the British Embassy in Ankara and changed the safes and their combinations, thus putting Cicero out of business.[2]

The exact sequence of events is clear. CICERO joined Sir Hughe's staff in September 1943. He volunteered his services to Moyzisch the following month, and in November von Papen sent a signal to Berlin which was subsequently passed by Kolbe to Dulles. The question is, on what date did Dulles first learn of CICERO's existence? It is impossible to establish this from the Swiss end because no record has been released detailing the exact dates of Kolbe's visits. According to OSS's *War Report*, declassified in 1976, 'For several months, "Wood" managed to go to Switzerland every few weeks.'[3] Furthermore, the process had been slowed down because 'the task of translating and encoding took the time of the entire staff at Bern for weeks after each batch of telegrams was received . . .'

What makes Dulles's recollection so interesting is that Moyzisch had been able to put a date on the new security measures imposed at the British Embassy:

As early as mid-January, Cicero told me, various men began arriving at the British Embassy from London, apparently engaged on mysterious errands. It seemed obvious to me that they were doing a security check-up, and I guessed that the British authorities suspected that the leakage was from somewhere inside their Embassy. Cicero told me that all the safes were being fitted with specially devised safety alarms.[4]

If one takes Dulles literally, and we accept that CICERO was 'put out of business' by his prompt intervention, the date of Kolbe's vital delivery of top-secret documents from the British Embassy in Ankara must have been around December 1943. Yet CICERO continued to be run as a spy by Moyzisch until March 1944. How could CICERO continue to operate for two months after the British had been alerted?

Those two inexplicable months were seized upon by many observers: around them myths flourished. Had the British known about CICERO all along? Had SIS been using him for purposes of deception?

The first doubts about CICERO's simple role as a spy

were voiced after the breaking of secrecy about ULTRA. If Bletchley had indeed been reading much of Nazi Germany's diplomatic cable traffic, how had CICERO remained undiscovered? Perhaps there was more to the story than first appeared from the Dulles account?

Revelations about ULTRA also encouraged several retired intelligence officers to break their long silences about their wartime work in the field of strategic deception. Some operations, like the famed Man Who Never Was, had been known about for many years. What had not been fully appreciated was the immense scale of the Allied deception effort and the lengths to which the various intelligence organizations were prepared to go to in order to dove-tail their operations with the objectives of other agencies. The fact that a special co-ordinating department, London Controlling Section, had even existed came as a surprise to many veterans. Widespread publicity about CICERO, about ULTRA, about deception, encouraged people to wonder whether CICERO was a triumph for British intelligence, and its subtle deception techniques, or simply an embarrassing breach of elementary security.

There was, indeed, a wealth of circumstantial evidence to support the deception idea. Some came from the Germans themselves. Although Moyzisch, CICERO's German controller, overcame his own initial doubts about the authenticity of CICERO's product, his superiors considered it too good to be true. Moyzisch described them as being 'the most carefully guarded secrets of the enemy, both political and military, and of incalculable value'.[5] Nevertheless, the German Foreign Office remained sceptical: 'As for the Cicero documents, Ribbentrop had examined them personally. He was still convinced that the whole thing was a British trap.'[6]

German doubts about CICERO had been fed by various discrepancies in the Albanian's story. He was found to have lied about his command of the English language, and the appearance of what looked like someone else's thumb on one photographic print seemed to contradict his claim to be working alone. The Germans were also dubious about the valet's stated motive: he was violently anti-British because an Englishman had shot his father. The circumstances of this incident changed each time CICERO mentioned it. Schellenberg, the former Sicherheitsdienst leader, later recalled:

I considered all this of incidental importance, but it did raise considerable difficulties in my proving to Hitler and Himmler the validity of 'Cicero's' material. Towards the end of December further doubts were thrown upon his veracity . . .[7]

Controversy on the whole CICERO subject surfaced again in March 1971 when Sir Hughe died and the risk of libel was eliminated. His obituary in the *Daily Telegraph* on 23 March 1971 mentioned that CICERO had made 'microfilms of the Allied D-Day invasion plans which he took from his employer's safe'.

This prompted Major-General Charles Swynnerton, who served as military attaché in Ankara in the 1950s, to write in on 14 April with what he called 'the whole story': 'Knowledge of a serious leak in security at Ankara had reached London in 1943, and Sir Knox Helm was sent there expressly to plug the leak in the British Embassy.'

Unfortunately Swynnerton's contribution muddied the water further, for he had mixed up Helm with another Foreign Office investigator. Clarification was needed, and Sir John Lomax, who had actually served on Sir Hughe's staff as Commercial Counsellor, joined the increasingly confused debate:

The Swynnerton version errs in important details. Helm was not sent to Ankara because of Foreign Office suspicions in 1943. His posting was in June 1942 – before the leakages began – and for quite different reasons.[8]

Unfortunately, in his enthusiasm for the subject, Lomax offered another red herring:

The fact of Cicero's spying only came to light after the war, when my opposite number in the German Embassy, who was the spy-master in disguise, fell into American hands and made his disclosures about Cicero under interrogation.

The matter might have rested there had not the controversial historian David Irving pointed out that German archives contained files which included certain summaries of intelligence from CICERO. Some even mentioned the code-word OVERLORD: General Jodl had remarked in his diary under the heading 'Results from Cicero': 'Overlord=Major invasion from Britain.'

Although CICERO's original reports were apparently lost, the numerous references to his information indicated that he had acquired vital secrets concerning the proposed Allied invasion, in spite of Swynnerton's protests to the contrary. Surely so sensitive a code-word would not have been deliberately compromised as part of an Allied deception campaign? Others pointed out that OVERLORD was only a preliminary code-word, which was subsequently dropped in favour of a series of operational code-words, such as NEPTUNE.

In 1976 Anthony Cave Brown turned his attention to these doubts and noticed that one member of Sir Hughe's staff, listed as an 'assistant military attaché', was 'Lieutenant-Colonel Montague Reaney Chidson, the former chief of MI6's continental secret service . . . and now a high executive of the British secret service in Turkey'.[9] Bearing in mind Chidson's true role, Cave Brown speculated, 'it is also possible that Chidson confronted Bazna and brought him under direct control'.[10]

Cave Brown's treatment of the CICERO case is remarkable because he appears to have got Dulles to contradict what Dulles had himself written earlier. For example, in neither *The Craft of Intelligence* nor *The Secret Surrender* does Dulles depart from his line that CICERO had been put out of business immediately. Yet in an interview Cave Brown quoted Dulles as saying that three days after he had informed the SIS representative in Berne, Count Vanden Heuvel, about CICERO, the SIS man had returned

'. . . and quite literally begged me to forget about the telegrams and take no action whatsoever about the Cicero case, particularly with Kolbe. Count Vanden Huyvel said London was "aware" of the case and, while Vanden Huyvel did not say so, it was obvious to me that the British were playing some sort of game with Cicero.'[11]

So in the three years between the publication of *The Secret Surrender* in 1966 and his death in January 1969 Dulles had apparently changed his story. Indeed, the interview claimed by Cave Brown must have taken place some six years before the publication of *Bodyguard of Lies*. This may well have happened, but there is no explanation of why Dulles contradicted his own previous accounts.

Cave Brown concludes his account by referring to 'the success of the Cicero deception'[12] and says:

The price paid for the Cicero stratagem was nominal. The British gave the Germans no intelligence which they could not obtain from other sources, and/or which they could not have obtained from accounts in the Allied and neutral press. And for those who still insisted that Cicero was a gigantic blunder, the final word must come from Menzies, who snapped, long after it really mattered what Bazna had or had not done, 'Of course Cicero was under our control.'

This was another remarkable quotation, for Menzies must have broken the habit of a lifetime to speak to a journalist. But, like Dulles, Menzies was dead when Cave Brown's quote was published, so he was not available to authenticate it.

Menzies's apparent endorsement of Cave Brown's theory that CICERO had been part of a brilliant Allied plot was welcomed by others, including Constantine Fitz-Gibbon, the American author who, coincidentally, had helped to translate Moyzisch's book a quarter of a century earlier. In 1976 FitzGibbon admitted in *Secret Intelligence in the Twentieth Century* that, 'The longer I worked on this job, the more sceptical did I become, not about the authenticity of Moyzisch's story but what lay behind it.'[13] FitzGibbon retold CICERO's story and then concluded: 'One can only conclude that the whole was an elaborate hoax, mounted by the Secret Intelligence Service to deceive the Germans . . .'[14]

Two years after FitzGibbon had published these words Sir Fitzroy Maclean reviewed the case in *Take Nine Spies* and added an ambiguous footnote:

It has naturally been suggested that Cicero was under British control throughout. On the evidence available this seems unlikely. According to Professor H. R. Trevor-Roper, however, who writes with authority and inside knowledge, Cicero had already been identified before he left the Embassy and for his final period of office there was used by British Intelligence 'to deceive instead of inform'.[15]

Such opinions firmly established the CICERO myth although, for once, the mythmakers had given the perfidious British Secret Service the credit for something they had never done.

The real facts, which have been confirmed to me by two former members of the Secret Intelligence Service's Station in Istanbul, both of whom served in the Section V, counter-intelligence section, and by Colonel Chidson's family, are quite different. CICERO was indeed a genuine spy who exploited Sir Hughe Knatchbull-Hugessen's appalling lack of personal security. Dulles did learn of the existence of a spy in the British Embassy in Ankara from copies of German telegrams provided by Fritz Kolbe (code-named GEORGE WOOD), but so too did the British. As the Franco-Swiss frontier was not opened to Allied traffic until September 1944, no letters were sent or delivered before that date; instead, all information for transmission abroad was enciphered and sent by wireless. In order to ensure their integrity during transmission from Geneva, the so-called GEORGE WOOD papers were divided equally between the British and Americans, half going to Washington, half to London.

However, none of the German cables actually identified the spy by name, merely by his code-name; so that, although the British were warned by Dulles and by information in their share of the GEORGE WOOD papers that they had a spy in their Embassy at Ankara, they still did not know who it was. A major investigation had to be undertaken first to discover his identity.

At the time the Foreign Office's Chief Security Officer was William Codrington, and he despatched his assistant, Sir John Dashwood, and a Special Branch detective, Chief Inspector Cochrane, to plug the leak. Unfortunately their enquiries merely served to tip off CICERO (and, as we have seen, Moyzisch). Nevertheless, CICERO was able to continue stealing Embassy secrets because Dashwood and Cochrane concentrated their efforts on the Embassy and not the ambassador's residence, where CICERO was employed. In fact, the two sleuths failed to identify Bazna as the source until after he had handed in his resignation and dropped from sight. By that time it was too late to take any action against him. Dashwood had to content himself by writing a withering condemnation of Sir Hughe's laxity for the eyes of the Foreign Secretary. As is the Foreign Office's custom, Sir Hughe's career did not appear to suffer and he went on to fulfil several important post-war positions. This in itself was enough for some to think that the absence of a public reprimand was an indication that Sir Hughe had been a participant in an elaborate deception campaign. In fact, it was another example of the Foreign Office protecting its own.

And the explanation of Chidson's mysterious presence in Ankara? Far from being the 'former chief of MI6's continental secret service' as portrayed by Cave Brown, Chidson had been recuperating from a nervous breakdown and had been posted to Ankara as a sinecure. His only covert role was that of the Embassy's Security Officer. Secret intelligence was left to his SIS colleagues at the Station in Istanbul. As it turned out, Chidson's sinecure proved too arduous a task, and a myth was created.

8
King Kong of Arnhem

Some of Lindemans's compatriots thought him to be a staunch member of the Dutch underground; but the Germans knew him in another capacity – as a spy. King Kong was a double agent. Lindemans had turned traitor in 1943.

CORNELIUS RYAN in *A Bridge Too Far*

In the past forty years many of the great mysteries of the last war have been resolved. The gradual release of official records and the declassification of some post-war documents have enabled historians to tie up dozens of the 'loose ends' which, for security and other reasons, could not be made public in the immediate post-war period. F. W. Winterbotham's revelation in 1974 of the scale of the Allied decryption operation prompted a comprehensive reassessment of the achievements of certain British and American commanders and, as we have seen, shed new light on particular incidents.

Since 1974 there have been a host of books dealing with the contribution made to the Allied prosecution of the war by the code-breakers based at Bletchley. Following Winterbotham's account large numbers of previously classified summaries of signals intelligence data have been released in England by the Public Record Office. In America too, the National Security Agency has declassified large quantities of historically significant information. There would seem to be few wartime secrets left, given the general acceptance of the view that wartime records now hold little current operational value or relevance.

Nevertheless, there are a small number of incidents and operations that raise the blood temperature of historians and still cause indignant letters to be written to newspapers. Occasionally such matters surface when someone takes on the role of mythmaker, and there are sufficient interested parties surviving to join battle over the issues raised.

One such controversy that has raged continuously since the conclusion of hostilities in Europe in 1945 concerns the secret intelligence operations conducted or supervised by the British in Nazi-occupied Holland. Long before Masterman's *The Double Cross System* had been published former Abwehr personnel had described in detail their counter-intelligence activities in Holland which had led to the almost total German domination and manipulation of the Allied networks. The basis of this extraordinary intelligence coup, which led to the deaths of more than a hundred Allied agents, was the 'working back' of a number of captured wireless sets.

The catastrophe undermined the Dutch government-in-exile's confidence in Britain's ability to conduct secret intelligence operations, and after the war a Dutch Parliamentary Commission of Enquiry was empanelled under the chairmanship of Dr L. A. Donker to ascertain what had gone wrong. Had there been negligence, treachery, or both? The Commission took evidence from everyone involved, including British, Dutch and German intelligence personnel, but although its final report managed to clear certain individuals of some wild charges, the recriminations continued. Rumour and speculation continue to this day, and each time some apparently relevant item of information is disclosed the debate is reopened. For example, soon after it had been revealed in 1979 that Anthony Blunt had confessed to having worked as a Soviet spy, the *Sunday Telegraph* published a bizarre story linking him to the capture and execution of nearly fifty agents sent to Holland by SOE's Dutch Section. It subsequently transpired that the newspaper had confused two separate Blunts: Anthony Blunt, who worked during the war for MI5, and the cover-name 'Blunt' used by a member of SOE's Dutch Section. Unsubstantiated allegations of treachery had been made against the SOE 'Blunt' (and some of his colleagues), and the revelation that another wartime intelligence officer bearing the same surname was a Soviet spy had been such a coincidence that inevitably someone had drawn the wrong inference. Whatever Anthony Blunt's crimes, complicity in SOE's affairs was not one of them. The *Sunday Telegraph* later admitted its error.

The friction caused by the German success in wartime Holland has now become legendary. A former CIA officer, Peer de Silva, recalled in *Sub Rosa: The CIA and the Uses of Intelligence* an extraordinary incident which, the author claimed, had occurred in the spring of 1953 when the Dutch Parliamentary Commission visited London to review British files:

> The delegation was met by British representatives, who coolly informed them that, unfortunately, within the past day there had been a 'serious fire' in the MI6 file room. By coincidence, all Dutch resistance records had been destroyed. In the light of this astounding piece of news, the Dutch immediately left on a return flight to The Hague. Shortly thereafter the Dutch government expelled the MI6 representative and his assistants and closed down the British intelligence station in The Hague.[1]

A truly remarkable business but, sadly for the mythmakers, an invention. In fact, the Dutch Parliamentary Commission had visited London in October 1949 and had been granted access to records and personnel. Nine senior SIS and SOE officers answered the Commission's questions and, two months later on 14

December, the British Foreign Office issued a statement, which insisted that

the suggestion that the lives of Dutch patriots were deliberately sacrificed in the interests of other objectives in the Netherlands, or elsewhere, is both repugnant to His Majesty's Government and the British people and entirely lacking in foundation.

Traditionally SIS and MI5 show their secrets to no one, be they Cabinet ministers, royalty or foreign parliamentarians. They simply conduct operations under broad ministerial guidance and circulate intelligence summaries or advice on particular issues when requested or required. Of the tiny handful of historians who have been granted access to SIS intelligence, each has himself been directly involved in intelligence work. Thus Professor M. R. D. Foot, the distinguished academic who was commissioned by the government to write the history of SOE in France, was himself a former Special Air Service officer who had operated behind the German lines in France in the days immediately before D-Day. Even so he was required to sign an undertaking never to reveal the location of SIS's Registry before he was allowed to enter SIS's Registry at Century House, where SOE's old records were stored. Similarly, every one of Professor Hinsley's team of three co-authors working on the official history of *British Intelligence in the Second World War* was a former intelligence officer. Hinsley himself had served as a code-breaker at Bletchley.

The mutual distrust displayed by the British and the Dutch intelligence organizations dates from the first moments that it was suspected that the Germans had managed to penetrate the security of the resistance networks in wartime Holland. There were, however, further incidents which took place after the conclusion of the débâcle, known in Abwehr circles as the England Spiel, which ended in March 1944 with a comic telegram sent from the Abwehr over an SOE wireless net which was operating under its control. The affair that served to increase the inter-service hostility and perpetuate the mistrust centred on Christiaan Lindemans, the Dutch resistance leader whose enormous size had caused him to be nick-named 'King Kong'.

Lindemans had been arrested on 28 October 1944 after it had been alleged that, far from a hero of the resistance, he had actually been a German spy and had betrayed the Allied plans to launch a massive airborne attack on Arnhem. Lindemans was interrogated by MI5 at the headquarters of the Combined Services Detailed Interrogation Centre at Latchmere House, Ham Common, for a fortnight and then returned to Dutch custody, where he remained until the end of July 1946, when he committed suicide in a prison hospital. He had never been charged or convicted of any crime, but his story, steeped in the intrigue that characterized Anglo-Dutch relations after April 1944, has become an essential wartime intelligence myth, and one of the few that is never likely to be resolved completely.

In 1944 Lindemans had turned up in Antwerp and offered his services to Colonel J. M. Langley, the local MI9 representative responsible for running escape routes for Allied servicemen who were trying to evade capture and get back to their own lines. Lindemans had been cleared for operational intelligence duties by 21st Army Group and was armed with impressive credentials as the leader of a Dutch resistance group. Four days before 17 September, when Operation MARKET GARDEN was launched on Arnhem, Lindemans was granted permission to cross the enemy's lines and establish contact with a group of Allied evaders who were thought to be hiding with the resistance in Eindhoven. Lindemans survived the experience, but was denounced and arrested soon after Eindhoven's liberation.

Although the British press had speculated in 1946 about the identity of a Dutch traitor who, they alleged, had been recently imprisoned in the Tower of London, little was said publicly about the Lindemans case until 1950, when Oreste Pinto wrote an article for the *Sunday Despatch*. Two years later Pinto's first book, *Spycatcher*, was published, giving details, in a chapter entitled 'The Traitor of Arnhem', of 'perhaps the most important spy-case in the whole history of espionage'.[2]

Pinto recalled how he had first encountered Lindemans, a twenty-seven-year-old ex-wrestler, at an Allied detention camp near Antwerp in 1944. Pinto had been the security officer at the camp and had reprimanded Lindemans for removing two women from the camp before they had been cleared for release. The incident had apparently led Pinto to investigate the resistance leader's background and to send a note warning of his suspicions to Langley. Nevertheless, Langley gave his approval to Lindemans's mission, which went ahead.

According to *Spycatcher*, Pinto called Lindemans in for interrogation shortly before Operation MARKET GARDEN, but Lindemans failed to appear because he had been attached to the Canadian forces for special duties. With perhaps more than an element of hindsight, Pinto suggested that to send Lindemans across enemy lines was equivalent to 'broadcasting the news of the forthcoming Allied parachute landings on the BBC news bulletins'.[3]

Pinto's warnings were all ignored, but six weeks after the Arnhem débâcle a self-confessed Abwehr agent named Cornelis Verloop denounced Lindemans as having alerted a German intelligence officer to the imminent attack. Pinto recalled the interrogation:

'Did King Kong betray Arnhem to the Nazis?' I asked. Verloop nodded . . . 'Yes, he told Colonel Kiesewetter on September 15, when he called at Abwehr headquarters. He said that British and American troops were to be dropped.'
'Did he say where?'
'Ja. He said a British airborne division was waiting to be dropped on Sunday morning beyond Eindhoven.'

Pinto then suggests that this evidence was enough proof for Lindemans to be arrested, and he also suggests that Lindemans then made a written statement confessing collaboration with the Abwehr, saying that he met 'Colonel Kiesewetter of the Abwehr at Driebergen on September 15, two days before the landings were to take place, and told him all the secret facts with which he had been entrusted'.[4]

However, when Pinto attempted to pursue Lindemans further he was discouraged and, to his astonishment, the dossier had vanished, in the best traditions of conspiracies:

. . . when I went to get the vital file it was not in its proper place. I searched carefully on neighbouring shelves and in nearby filing cabinets in case it had been accidentally filed away in the wrong place. There was no sign of it.[5]

Pinto was then transferred out of the Dutch Security Service and posted to new duties in Germany. These strange events persuaded Pinto that the Dutch government was anxious to suppress what was fast becoming the scandal of the Lindemans affair.

Apart from Pinto's testimony, the chief reason for believing that MARKET GARDEN had been betrayed was the failure of the operation itself. The original plan went awry from the moment the first paratroopers hit the ground at Arnhem and encountered no less than two crack SS armoured divisions in and around the dropping zone. But was the presence of the 9th and 10th Panzer divisions evidence of a carefully prepared trap or simply poor reconnaissance by the Allies? The betrayal theory, combined with Pinto's word, seemed a distinct possibility.

However, in 1953 one of the Abwehr officers responsible for masterminding the England Spiel, Hermann Giskes, published an account of it in *London Calling North Pole*. In this book he revealed that he had been the person responsible for recruiting Lindemans as an agent. He also explained that, although Lindemans knew that English and American troops were standing by for a big airborne operation soon, he did not know where they were hoping to land. Giskes said that he

never found out what King Kong reported to the IC of the German general headquarters in Vught when he was taken there on the afternoon of 14th September; but he did pass his knowledge on to Major Wieskotter in Driebergen on the 15th. In any case there was no mention of Arnhem – King Kong had not mentioned it probably because he simply did not know in what area the airborne attack was going to be made.[6]

Giskes explained that although he was perfectly satisfied with his agent's reliability, to the officer in command of the German General Staff in Holland Lindemans 'was simply a suspicious foreigner who could well have been sent across for deception purposes'.

According to Giskes the Wehrmacht had other reasons for supposing that an Allied airborne attack was imminent. One important source was signals intelligence: 'The traffic heard on 15th September was a conclusive indication of the imminence of a large-scale enemy air operation.'[7]

Giskes concluded that Lindemans 'was not the betrayer of Arnhem, simply because he was not in a position to betray it!'

However if Pinto is correct, Lindemans may have thought his warning of an airborne attack was sufficient to betray the whole operation, hence the signed confession.

In 1969 Anne Laurens wrote a highly partisan and controversial study on the subject, *The Lindemans Affair*, and came to a startling conclusion: King Kong had been a British double agent and had been the conduit for a complicated Allied deception plan. The perfidious British secret services, having recruited him into a complex counter-intelligence operation, had eventually found it politically expedient to abandon Christiaan Lindemans to his fate.

The Abwehr had poisoned so many networks that they no longer knew where they were. It was imperative that they retaliate by infiltrating an agent into Colonel Giskes' organization. A double agent who would arrive telling such a plausible story that the Germans would swallow it completely. Finally, the last most diabolical stroke, a double was needed who could be sacrificed if need be, if the operation went wrong or if his services became useless, a double therefore who could not pride himself on having many influential relationships.[8]

Although Anne Laurens was unable to identify the Allied officers responsible for engaging Lindemans as a double agent, she was convinced of the role they had played:

They had only forgotten one thing, these Machiavellian leaders, and that was to warn Christiaan that if ever someone from his side accused him of treason, nobody would lift a finger to help him. Indeed, if necessary, they would plunge him in deeper, if it served their purposes.[9]

Laurens also took a dim view of Pinto and alleged that he and Lindemans had not clashed over a security matter, but over women. In *Spycatcher* Pinto had often referred to Lindemans's 'countless amours and intrigues'[10] and described how he had become 'famed for his sexual prowess'.[11] Lindemans had apparently been a 'superb muscular athlete with a reputation for turning girls' heads'.[12] Laurens interpreted these comments as a manifestation of prurient hypocrisy and criticized Pinto's condemnation of Lindemans's sexual escapades:

A curious moral judgement by a man whose private life was, to say the least, stormy. He, himself, had been accused by his superiors of having had intimate relations with women 'with whom he dropped his guard', even though they were, beyond doubt, enemy agents.[13]

Pinto died in September 1961 so there was no risk of legal action over such a libellous accusation. Nevertheless, no evidence was offered to support the allegation, beyond the repetition of what was admitted to be merely a rumour: 'It was whispered that in addition to the animosity that had already sprang up between them, they added a certain amount of rivalry with their women which did not help matters.'

Laurens was convinced that Pinto had had an ulterior motive for doubting Lindemans's loyalty and claimed: 'Pinto swore that he would not rest until he had proved the allegations that he had really only thrown at random under the influence of his jealous temper.'[14]

Whatever Laurens's reservations about Pinto and his motives, she was obliged to come to terms with his account of Lindemans's signed confession. Pinto had already described the statement as 'a full and detailed confession covering twenty-four pages of closely-typed foolscap'.[15] The Dutch counter-espionage expert remembered that he had actually taken 'the top secret confession to my office and sat down to study it. It was more exciting than any detective story and it was satisfying to read the confirmation of much guess-work and deduction.'

But Laurens had a different version of the confession and Pinto's account:

According to Colonel Pinto, Christiaan then gave detailed statements, filling up twenty-four foolscap pages, each page initialled by 'the accused'. But the British refused to part with the Lindemans file and only furnished the Dutch Security Office with extracts.[16]

The differences between the two versions are obvious, but what is more interesting is the bias of the authors. Pinto thought the Dutch government was behind the conspiracy to cover up the Lindemans affair. Laurens, on the other hand, had manipulated the facts to make the British the villains of the piece. On one occasion, though, she let her guard slip and suggested that, following some internal political disputes among the various Dutch resistance groups, 'it was decided to sacrifice Christiaan Lindemans as he now knew too much about the "England Spiel". It was now merely a question of waiting for the right time.'[17]

By accepting that Lindemans had made a confession concerning Arnhem, Laurens was obliged to offer a convoluted explanation. Lindemans, it seems, did betray details of MARKET GARDEN, but only because he had been ordered to: 'Obeying the orders of his superiors, he had given Kiesewetter the information about "Operation Market Garden", prepared by the Allies for the Abwehr, only two days before the operation was launched.'[18]

Once again the central conflict with Giskes is high-lighted. Giskes, as we know, had been adamant that he had never received any information concerning Arnhem from Lindemans. So how could Laurens not only insist that he had, but that he had done so on British instructions? This inconsistency had not escaped Laurens, who found an explanation in Giskes's alleged vanity:

Whether Giskes admitted to himself that he was betrayed by his 'man of confidence' is not important. Giskes, as seen from his memoirs, liked to stretch out the number of his successes, and did not voluntarily admit having been fooled. He only admitted it when it was impossible not to.

If Giskes had suffered from such vanity (and such a charge cannot be substantiated), surely he would have been more inclined to take the easier course and claim he had obtained vital intelligence from Lindemans? An admission that his trusted agent had failed to convey this crucial information can hardly be portrayed as a success. Nevertheless, this is the view of Anne Laurens.

Quite apart from Giskes's recollection, there is other evidence available to support the contention that Lindemans could not have betrayed Arnhem. General Kurt Student, for example, who was on the scene at the time, is quoted as saying 'nobody in the German command knew anything about the attack until it happened'. In any event the two SS Panzer divisions which were regrouping at Arnhem at the time of MARKET GARDEN had begun to congregate there well before the Allies had even drawn up their plans. Furthermore, the final details for the attack had not been completed until after Lindemans had set off on his mission into enemy territory.

In 1966, in *Akin to Treason*, John Bulloch seemed to take the Pinto line a stage further:

The Germans knew from other Intelligence reports and from their observation of the activity going on behind the British lines that an attack was imminent, but they had not suspected that airborne forces would be used, nor had they imagined that Arnhem would be attacked. Lindemans must bear a heavy responsibility for the frightful losses suffered by the British airborne divisions at Arnhem.[20]

With reports such as these it is hardly surprising that Lindemans's own British contact ended up believing that he might have contributed to the Arnhem débâcle. In 1974, in *Fight Another Day*, Colonel J. M. Langley, the former MI9 officer who had authorized Lindemans's mission, recalled his brief acquaintanceship with his Dutch agent:

He asked to be sent through the lines near Eindhoven to collect evaders he was sure would be hiding with his resistance friends in that area. The relevant Army Group intelligence section had already checked King Kong's credentials and had reported 'nothing known against'. The Dutch Army commander agreed to the mission but the head of their counter-espionage section, Colonel Oreste Pinto, sent me a private warning that he believed it possible that King Kong was a German agent though as yet he had no proof. For King Kong's subsequent action I must accept responsibility.[21]

Langley stated that he had been the subject of an official enquiry, but had been exonerated thanks to the security clearance issued by 21st Army Group. Nevertheless, the enquiry felt that Langley 'should have taken Colonel Pinto's warning more seriously'. The enquiry also established that Lindemans 'had been in contact with individuals who knew of plans to use the British and American airborne divisions but that he could not possibly have discovered the actual dropping zones'.[22]

Langley maintained, correctly, that intelligence gathered later had confirmed the view that Lindemans had not betrayed MARKET GARDEN. Indeed, Lindemans's notorious visit to Abwehr headquarters on 15 September had anyway resulted in a report which 'had been dismissed as of no import'.

Langley undoubtedly looked back on the Lindemans affair with a clear conscience, although he declared it had been 'a narrow escape'.[23] If Langley was justified in his opinion, then Pinto's story of a confession must be flawed. And since Anne Laurens concedes Lindemans did pass on intelligence relevant to MARKET GARDEN (albeit for the most patriotic of motives), her version must be categorized as speculation. We know from Giskes that King Kong had acted as an Abwehr agent since his recruitment in 1943. We know too that he was never in a position to betray Arnhem, even if he might have wanted to, or even if he thought he actually had. It has also been established beyond reasonable doubt that the Germans had no foreknowledge of MARKET GARDEN. But given the feuding and mutual distrust that seems to have characterized relations between the Allies and the Dutch resistance groups in the autumn of 1944, the entire affair is bound to remain a profitable area of growth for the mythologists.

9

Nuremberg: The Double Cross

The Germans did not identify the target until long after they had made contact with the bomber stream – a fact which disposes of the rumour that information had been leaked to them – and if the raid was a disaster for Bomber Command it was because the risk of fighter interception was gravely underestimated.

F. H. HINSLEY in *British Intelligence in the Second World War*[1]

The details of the RAF's raid on Nuremberg on the night of 30/31 March 1944 are well documented, as are the disastrous consequences. The Allies lost a total of 745 airmen killed and a further 159 wounded or taken prisoner. The exact number of aircraft lost is still unknown because many listed as having returned made such poor landings, owing in the main to flak damage, that they were later scrapped. Nevertheless, the probable figure is 170 planes destroyed, compared with the Luftwaffe's losses of less than ten. There can be little dispute that the disaster was the worst of the war for the RAF, which suffered heavier casualties during this single raid than during the entire period of the Battle of Britain.

These horrific statistics are a matter of historical record, but the question remains, how could such a catastrophe have happened? The German ground defences and the Luftwaffe nightfighters wrought havoc among the bomber force, so much so that several surviving pilots declared angrily during their debriefing that 'they must have known we were coming'. The scene must have been reminiscent of Mountbatten's post-mortem after the JUBILEE débâcle.

In retrospect it is clear that if the object of the Nuremberg raid had been to lure the Luftwaffe into a major air battle, and a major air defeat, the exercise can be seen to have been a tragic failure. Arguments concerning Bomber Command's strategic objectives on the night of the raid are likely to continue for some years, but the intelligence angle must be examined in detail.

In 1976, in *Bodyguard of Lies*, Anthony Cave Brown came up with a typically controversial explanation. Not only did the Germans demonstrably have foreknowledge of the operation, but that information had been leaked deliberately: 'to establish the credibility of a double agent cannot be discounted'.[2]

Cave Brown claimed that there were numerous operational advantages to be taken by such a stratagem, bearing in mind that 'the raid was, by its very nature, sacrificial'. By using an agent who was already operating under Allied Control as a conduit, the Germans could have been fed the exact details concerning the RAF's future targets; this would make the agent providing all this detail seem exceptionally knowledgeable and reliable. He would thus become a valuable vehicle for British deception.

Operation FORTITUDE was the Allied masterplan to deceive the enemy and distract them from the coastline selected for the D-Day landings. FORTITUDE was a comprehensive plan involving a variety of weapons: dummy landing-craft on the east coast, all apparently gathered in anticipation of an amphibious assault across the North Sea; poorly camouflaged concentrations of troops and armour in East Anglia; sloppy wireless security in south-east England, enabling German direction-finding stations to locate hastily established but temporary army quarters. And one significant branch of the FORTITUDE deception was the use of the direct channel of communication with the enemy offered by the stable of double agents operated under the supervision of the Security Service, MI5.

There is, not surprisingly, very little evidence from official sources to support the idea that Churchill ordered a double agent to betray one of the RAF's targets. Cave Brown quotes a remark made by Masterman – 'The larger the prize the higher must also be the preliminary stake' – as proof that the Security Service was prepared to take considerable risks to achieve an important goal. Cave Brown also identifies the two agents most likely to have been used to convey the news concerning the Nuremberg raid: 'If a double agent was used to warn the Germans of the Nuremberg attack, Garbo or Brutus would have been logical choices.'

Because GARBO and BRUTUS are the two candidates put forward by Cave Brown, their activities should now be examined.

Both GARBO and BRUTUS started their work as double agents for MI5 in the same year, 1942. BRUTUS was well known to the British authorities, having run a very successful network, known as the INTERALLIE ring, in Paris after the Nazi occupation in 1940. His real name was Roman Garby-Czerniawski, a Polish air-officer who happened to have been attending a training course in France when the war had broken out. In November 1941 Garby-Czerniawski had been betrayed by a member of his own network and had been arrested by the Germans. He later described his experiences in *The Big Network*. After a period of imprisonment in Fresnes, the Pole had been offered a deal by the Abwehr. If he travelled to England to spy for the Abwehr, all the members of his organization would be spared a firing squad and treated as prisoners of war. Garby-Czerniawski had accepted and, in October 1942, had reported to the British Embassy in Madrid for repatriation to England, posing as an escapee. He had been interrogated on his arrival in London, but his reputation as a resistance leader in France had travelled before him. It was only after he had been cleared for new duties at the Polish headquarters in London that he had revealed to the Polish Director of Military Intelligence the exact nature of the arrangement he had come to with the Abwehr. The Poles had consulted MI5, and Garby-Czerniawski had agreed to operate a wireless set 'in harness' on condition it did not jeopardize members of his ring who were still imprisoned in France. Dubbed BRUTUS by MI5, he was assigned The Hon. Hugh Astor as his case officer and together they had maintained a regular radio schedule with the Abwehr until January 1945, when the French authorities had tracked down those responsible for betraying the INTERALLIE network and had showed signs of putting them on public trial for collaborating with the enemy. MI5 believed that if the trials went ahead, there was a danger that BRUTUS might be called to give evidence. Such a development might have compromised the status of BRUTUS in the eyes of his German controllers, who, even at that late stage in the war, had been full of confidence about their loyal spy. Both Garby-Czerniawski and his case officer were still communicating to the Abwehr in 1944 at the time of the Nuremberg raid, as Cave Brown suggests.

Juan Pujol (GARBO), on the other hand, came to the attention of the British authorities under quite different circumstances. He was a Spanish idealist who had offered his services to SIS as a spy twice, once to the British Embassy in Madrid, and again via the American naval attaché in Lisbon. He had been turned down on both occasions, so he had arranged to be recruited by the

Germans instead. The Abwehr obtained confirmation from the Spanish that Pujol had indeed deserted the Republicans to join Franco's forces, and therefore accepted his claim to be a Nazi sympathizer. After some training in the latest espionage techniques Pujol was despatched to Portugal, apparently en route to England. Although Pujol reported his safe arrival to his Abwehr controller in July 1941, he had in fact got no further than Cascais, a fishing village near Lisbon. Nevertheless, the Germans took his subsequent reports at face value and seemed to believe that he had begun to develop a network of sub-agents in various strategic locations around the British Isles. However, unbeknownst to either Pujol or his German controller, these reports were intercepted by the British who routinely monitored all the enemy wireless traffic between Madrid and Berlin. A major investigation was launched to identify the Abwehr's new spy ring but, not surprisingly, the Security Service could find no trace of it. In fact, they eventually established that the network's information was pure fiction, but there remained a small threat to British security because the imaginary reports sometimes came uncomfortably close to the truth. The Allies also became increasingly anxious that the Germans might at some stage discover the deception and realize the ease with which they could be taken in. MI5 therefore sought, and received, permission to recruit him as an agent, and accordingly an SIS officer smuggled Pujol, his wife and son to Gibraltar, and then flew them to Plymouth late in April 1942. There they were met by Tomas Harris, a member of MI5's Iberian Section, B21. He escorted them to London and installed them in a safe-house in Crespigny Road, Hendon.

Tommy Harris and Juan Pujol (now dubbed GARBO) developed a truly remarkable relationship, with the MI5 case officer virtually taking over the personae of many of the sub-agents claimed by the Spanish double agent. GARBO himself pretended to pursue a career as a BBC translator, while Harris helped him to compile long and detailed reports for transmission to the Abwehr. A special wireless station was constructed on the roof of MI5's London headquarters and an operator from the Radio Security Service, Charles Haines, kept up a regular schedule with Madrid.

Once again, the allegation is that Tommy Harris collaborated in transmitting a warning to the Abwehr concerning the Nuremberg raid.

Those with a direct knowledge of the GARBO case are few in number because Harris and his direct superior, Dick Brooman-White, are both dead. GARBO himself is still alive and lives in quiet retirement in South America. Despite the passage of time he can recall many of the messages he sent, and he remains adamant on this issue: at no time in the war did he ever acquire a source with access to Bomber Command's operational targets. As a Polish staff officer Garby-Czerniawski was in a better position to obtain such information, but he is adamant that he did not, as is his case officer. Can they be believed?

One of the problems skated over by Cave Brown concerns the practical difficulties faced by a double agent conveying intelligence to the Abwehr. In the case of the Nuremberg raid, the target was only announced to his own staff by Air Chief Marshal 'Bomber' Harris on the morning of the raid. Even if an agent was able, against the odds, to gain access to the target chosen for that night, he could not simply start transmitting a message on his radio whenever he felt like it. Every wireless agent (and both GARBO and BRUTUS fell into this group) kept to a prearranged schedule which did not necessarily involve a daily transmission. Neither GARBO nor

BRUTUS transmitted on a daily basis. They might have had to wait for up to a fortnight before their next 'net' with the Abwehr was scheduled.

Indignant denials from BRUTUS and his case officer might be expected, as can the disavowal of Roger Hesketh, one of the authors of the FORTITUDE plan. In addition, there is not one surviving member of the Twenty Committee who is prepared to countenance the suggestion that a deliberate sacrifice had been made to build up the reputations of these two agents. It will be recalled that the Twenty Committee was set up specifically to co-ordinate the intelligence being passed to the enemy. They also point out the practical dangers of creating such a risky precedent. If a highly valued agent had demonstrated his ability to learn the RAF's secrets once, would not the Abwehr require further nuggets in the future? On such a slippery slope the entire system might be jeopardized. But had not Cave Brown actually quoted Masterman on the need to risk high stakes for the best results? Actually Cave Brown exercised a degree of selection when he chose that particular part of a sentence. The full context clarifies Masterman's meaning and shows that he was discussing the principles behind the running of double agents, and the difficulties in building them, sometimes over a period of years, from a liability into an asset:

An examination of subsequent chapters will show how this process has been carried out in a variety of cases; for the present it suffices to stress the obvious truth that the larger the prize the higher must also be the preliminary stake. In point of fact, however, the price paid has usually not been so very great after all, for many cases have been firmly established without giving away anything especially secret or important.[3]

So, far from advocating a heavy investment in a suitable agent, as Cave Brown's brief quote suggests, Masterman is actually putting the opposite view: an agent can become a valuable agent without handing vital secrets to the enemy. Once again, there is the question of the standing of the individual agents in the eyes of their German controllers. Was there ever a need to enhance their reputation? Not according to the Twenty Committee, who deliberated on this point when choosing suitable double agents to convey the FORTITUDE deceptions. Masterman says of GARBO:

In the early months of 1944 secret sources indicated clearly that GARBO and TRICYCLE were the most highly thought of, but their relative value oscillated, probably according not only to the information they gave, but also according to the claims made for them by their own spy-masters.[4]

The 'secret sources' to which Masterman refers is the interception and successful decryption of the Enigma-based Abwehr wireless traffic which was circulated within MI5 in the form of summaries bearing the code-name ISOS. The existence of ISOS remained a secret until 1981, long after ULTRA had been written about, and long after the publication of *Bodyguard of Lies*. ISOS information told Masterman that there was no need to build up GARBO since MI5 was able to monitor his progress through German eyes. As for BRUTUS in 1944, Masterman says:

In January, after considerable hesitation, it was decided that BRUTUS should be used for the same purpose [strategic deception] since secret sources revealed that our fears of German mistrust in him were not justified.[5]

So the reputation of BRUTUS was not in need of any artificial support at the relevant moment either. But if double agents played no part in the Nuremberg raid, what did cause the disaster? Professor R. V. Jones, SIS's scientific adviser, stated his view on the subject in *Most Secret War*, where he points out that the transmissions from the bombers alone would have warned the enemy of when an attack was likely to be mounted, 'in the failure of any effective diversion and in the general conditions obtaining that night, the losses were only to be expected'.[6]

Martin Middlebrook has also enquired into the disaster in *The Nuremberg Raid*. He agrees with Professor Jones that there were a number of factors which might have warned the Germans, including the weather. It was a clear night, ideal for the Luftwaffe night-fighters and the flak batteries on the ground. The half moon would also have illuminated the condensation trails left by the bombers, making them easy targets. Signals intelligence also probably played an important role. German interception of Bomber Command's radio signals during the routine pre-flight testing of plane-board equipment would have been enough to warn that a large collection of aircraft were massing. This testing was usually carried out before the fuel had been loaded and was the subject of blanket monitoring by the Germans.

As Professor Jones has highlighted, the RAF's diversionary tactics failed miserably on the night of the raid. Two separate groups of aircraft were sent to Germany, of which one was a decoy designed to mislead the enemy defences. There is now evidence to show that the Germans were quickly able to detect which of the two were using the H2S precision bombing radar and to conclude which was the major attack force. Once the ground defences had eliminated the decoy, they were able to plan a reception as the raiders moved deeper into German airspace.

Such an explanation is less dramatic than a straightforward betrayal, and is unlikely to contribute to any myths, but it is clearly the most plausible interpretation. The science of intelligence analysis is the piecing together of many different segments of information, rather than total reliance on a single source. The overall picture is gained by interlocking a series of small pieces together until the final picture shows a completed intelligence jigsaw puzzle and not a myth.

10

A Man Called Intrepid?

I must admit I am as baffled as you are surprised that Mr Stevenson has quoted us in print as having BSC Papers, as none clearly exist in the material we have so far received.
The University of Regina archivist in a letter to the author concerning *Intrepid's Last Case*, 22 March 1984

At the conclusion of the Second World War some British Intelligence officers were invited to write brief accounts of their wartime work for the historical record. These internal histories were never intended to be published, although one or two such authors retained their own private copies and occasionally these accounts have surfaced. Roger Hesketh, one of the key deception planners of D-Day, called his secret history *Fortitude* after the principal code-name for the Allied deception campaign executed in the weeks before the Normandy landings. A limited number of copies, all marked Top Secret, were printed by the Foreign Office, and Hesketh retained two of them. In 1968 much of the information contained in *Fortitude* appeared in Sefton Delmer's *The Counterfeit Spy*. Hesketh had not been consulted about Delmer's book, but when he objected to its publication he discovered that the Crown claimed ownership of the copyright. After a long legal wrangle, which failed to prevent the publication of an English edition, Delmer's book was withdrawn from sale in the United States.

Another secret wartime history written for the Security Service appeared in 1972 when J. C. Masterman published *The Double Cross System in the War of 1939–1945*. Masterman had been invited to record the activities of the Twenty Committee soon after the ending of hostilities, and had kept a copy which he arranged to publish in the United States. MI5 was enraged and attempted to block the publication, but Masterman won the day and obtained Prime Minister Edward Heath's consent to his plan.

Four years later, in 1976, another secret departmental history surfaced with the announcement that a forthcoming book by the Canadian author William Stevenson, entitled *A Man Called Intrepid*, had been based on what he referred to as 'the BSC Papers', a set of official documents tracing the activities of British Security Coordination in New York between 1940 and 1945. According to Sir William Stephenson, the former head of British Security Co-ordination, the papers 'consisted of many thick volumes and exhibits, covering five years of intense activity and thousands of operations across the world'.[1] Indeed, it was known that Dick Ellis, Stephenson's wartime deputy, had collaborated in the preparation of just such a summary immediately after the war for the Registry of the Secret Intelligence Service. The prospect of further disclosures in the mould of Masterman caused alarm in official quarters in London and the Cabinet's Intelligence Co-ordinator, Sir Dick White, sought, apparently unsuccessfully, to establish the whereabouts of Stevenson's 'vast records'.

Dick Ellis died on 5 July 1975. But *A Man Called Intrepid* appeared with a handsome Preface by Ellis in which he authenticated the text and confirmed that he had placed his own collection of papers at Stevenson's disposal.

There are, however, some disconcerting points concerning Dick Ellis's preface, in which he makes some surprising errors, including several mistakes about his own career. The most obvious inconsistency is Ellis's claim that H. Montgomery Hyde's first biography of Sir

William Stephenson, *The Quiet Canadian*, had received official support because the authorities were anxious to compensate for the defection of Kim Philby: 'I can now disclose that the reason for the break in the silence about BSC in 1962 was the escape to the Soviet Union of Kim Philby.'[2] This seems particularly odd, bearing in mind that Montgomery Hyde's book was published in November 1962 – a clear two months before Philby's escape in January 1963.

Dick Ellis had originally joined His Majesty's Consular Service in Istanbul in 1921 but, in 1923, he transferred into SIS, having been recommended for recruitment by the Head of Station in Paris, Major T. M. Langton. His appointment to the SIS post of Assistant Passport Control Officer in Berlin was confirmed in a letter dated 24 October 1923 from the headquarters of the Secret Intelligence Service in London to the Foreign Office. Yet in his preface Ellis states that he had been 'twenty years in the professional secret intelligence service when in 1940 London sent me to British Security Co-ordination headquarters in New York'. He had actually only been nearly seventeen years in the service by then. Perhaps this error can be explained by consulting *Who's Who*, which refers to 'various consular posts since 1921'. To someone familiar with the traditional diplomatic cover given to SIS officers, such a description might suggest that Ellis had indeed joined SIS in 1921. But the truth is that Ellis spent two years genuinely working as an acting vice-consul before his transfer to SIS.

It seems remarkable that Ellis was prepared to break the recognized convention whereby SIS officers, retired and active, avoid admitting their covert role. Such an admission from Ellis is especially surprising when one considers that in 1967 he confessed to having sold SIS secrets to the Germans before the war. No action was taken against him, and the pension which he had received since his retirement in 1953 continued to be paid. To have endorsed a book on the subject of espionage would certainly have meant placing his pension in jeopardy and may have risked the goodwill of the authorities upon which his freedom depended.

The effect of Dick Ellis's name on the preface to *A Man Called Intrepid* is to give the book an *imprimatur*. However, the book itself contains some inexplicable discrepancies. Either the author did not have easy access to Ellis's wartime history, or perhaps Ellis died before the final proofs were available for him to read. The preface written by Ellis is sufficient to ensure that the events described in the book are in danger of being taken as gospel and thus give rise to further myths.

The first myth concerns the code-name of the first Director of British Security Co-ordination, William Stephenson, and the telegraphic address of his organization. Both appear to have got a little muddled. In July 1940 the diminutive Canadian financier was sent to head the SIS Station in Manhattan as a replacement for Captain Sir James Paget RN. Paget, whose mother had been an American, was then approaching his fiftieth birthday and was recalled to London. Stephenson was six years younger and had been requested to cement Anglo-American relations. Stephenson had been a flying ace in the Great War and had subsequently made several fortunes as an industrialist. In the late 1930s he had been responsible for several important reports on the manufacture of German steel for Desmond Morton's Industrial Intelligence Centre in London. Until 1935 the Industrial Intelligence Centre had been a one-man bureau forwarding strategic information to the Board of Overseas Trade and, whenever necessary, to SIS's economic intelligence section. Among Morton's clients were a few leading politicians, including Winston Churchill.

Although Stephenson had never been an SIS officer, he was chosen to take command of SIS's affairs in the United States; under his direction the Manhattan Station grew to take in five separate divisions, each reflecting a different intelligence interest. The Secret Intelligence Division was headed by his Deputy Director, Dick Ellis. The remaining four were: Special Operations (headed by Ingram Fraser, and responsible for liaising with SOE in London); Economic Warfare (headed by John Pepper, formerly a London businessman); Political Warfare (headed by Cedric Belfrage); and Defence Security (headed by W. T. 'Freckles' Wren).

The most politically sensitive aspect of Stephenson's mission was his liaison with the US authorities, which were, of course, then still neutral. It was believed in London that a well-connected Canadian like Stephenson would have a better chance of 'speaking the same language' to the Americans and thereby of gaining their trust. This he achieved brilliantly. He developed a lasting friendship with William ('Wild Bill') Donovan, the man chosen by President Roosevelt to create an American intelligence organization, and established a training camp just over the border in Canada to train US personnel in British intelligence techniques. By exerting his influence over Donovan's embryonic unit, which later became known as the Office of Strategic Services, Stephenson acquired a unique position and made an extraordinary contribution to the intelligence war conducted by the Allies. After the war he was knighted for his work, and the US government rewarded him with the Medal of Merit.

In *A Man Called Intrepid* it is suggested that when the financier was sent to run the SIS Station he was granted the individual code-name INTREPID, which was given to him personally: 'Churchill felt strongly about code-names,' the book says, recording the moment that the Prime Minister selected Stephenson's: 'he added that the man to bring in the Americans must be fearless. He paused. "Dauntless?" He searched for the right word while Stephenson waited. "You must be – intrepid!" '[3] This seems unlikely as INTREPID was the actual cable address of British Security Co-ordination, an office located in the Rockefeller Center at 630 Fifth Avenue. It was registered as such with Western Union. Stephenson himself was assigned the code-number 48100, which indicated to SIS headquarters in London that telegrams bearing that figure had come from the SIS Head of Station in New York. All SIS Stations around the world identified themselves by an ingenious system of five-figure numbers. The first two digits indicated the country. The following two digits identified individual members of the Station staff. Thus 200 was invariably the Deputy Head of Station (in this case Dick Ellis) and 500 was the Section V representative. Agents run by these officers were always referred to in communications by the last two digits. If a message to London signed by 48900 mentioned a recent meeting with 48903 who was scheduled to sail to THIRTYSIXLAND, the meaning was instantly clear to those indoctrinated in the system. The system had come from Bill Ross-Smith, one of Stephenson's case officers. His agent 48903 would soon be visiting Sweden.

Because American law required all those working for foreign governments to register with the State Department, there was relatively little secrecy about the existence of the British Security Co-ordination office in New York, which was a matter of public record in Washington. The cable address, INTREPID, NEW YORK, was equally available in any cable office. But the significant point is that the word INTREPID referred to the organization rather than its Director. In other words, if 48100 was visiting London, telegrams to BSC were still addressed to INTREPID.

A further misunderstanding seems to have occurred over the choice of the code-name ULTRA for the secret decrypts from Bletchley. As is now well known, the wartime Bletchley cryptologists succeeded in solving a number of the German's ciphers using the Enigma cipher machine. In *A Man Called Intrepid* it is suggested that

a mechanical contrivance was built that reduced the work of the mathematicians. It would be some time before the enemy's secrets were laid bare by retrieving the German High Command's orders on a reasonably regular basis. But there was a sense of breakthrough, sufficient for Stephenson to propose that intelligence distilled from this source be labelled 'Top-secret Ultra'.[4]

But the classification ULTRA SECRET was not introduced until June 1941, more than twelve months later. Furthermore, the first Bletchley decrypts were disguised as information from an SIS agent code-named BONIFACE. This subterfuge was abandoned after the Directors of Air and Military Intelligence appeared to be ignoring GCHQ's material, and the prefix CX introduced. All the GCHQ's decrypts addressed to the Air Ministry and the War Office were channelled via SIS and bore the classification CX/TOP SECRET. Before June 1941 the Naval Intelligence Division (NID) maintained its own direct lines to GCHQ and referred to the intercepted intelligence as HYDRO. After June 1941 the NID scrapped HYDRO and also adopted the term ULTRA SECRET.[5]

The revelation of GCHQ's extraordinary achievements have led many people to reinterpret some important wartime events. In Chapter 1 of this book I have endeavoured to scotch the myth, that reoccurs in *A Man Called Intrepid*, that the GCHQ code-breakers intercepted the order which identified Coventry as the Luftwaffe's target for 14 November 1940. It is also suggested that Stephenson kept the American President informed on the German military situation following the evacuation of Dunkirk through Bletchley, although this could not have been possible, because GCHQ could only decrypt the Luftwaffe's Enigma keys at this time. The Wehrmacht's Enigma traffic was not broken until 1942, as the official history makes clear: '. . . months were still to elapse before the Naval Enigma, like the Army Enigma, could be read currently or in large amounts.'[6] Stevenson also implies that the code-breakers were so successful during the early summer of 1940 that 'ULTRA retrieved Hitler's invasion plans and their cover name, SEALION',[7] yet Professor Hinsley's history is quite clear on this point: 'On 21 September the Enigma vouchsafed the code word SEALION for the first time.'[8]

Whether the author of *A Man Called Intrepid* misunderstood his source material, or whether he relied on information other than that provided by Dick Ellis, is almost impossible to determine. While stationed in New York during the war Ellis had come into weekly contact with J. Edgar Hoover's local representative, Percy J. Foxworth. Yet this FBI officer is referred to in the book as Sam Foxforth. A small slip perhaps, but when enough occur they undermine the book's authenticity.

The photographs too give the wrong impression. Of a total of forty-three, forty are said to have come 'from the BSC Papers, Station M Archives'. In fact, fourteen are movie stills from *School for Danger*, a feature film made at Pinewood Studios after the war. Four had already been published in H. Montgomery Hyde's biographies

The Quiet Canadian and *Cynthia*. One came from a map annotated by the historian Professor M. R. D. Foot in 1962 for his book *SOE in France*, which was published in 1966. Another, a photographic portrait of Noor Inayat Khan, the SOE agent code-named MADELEINE, resembles an illustration from Jean Overton Fuller's biography, published in 1952. Finally, an enlargement of a photograph portraying Kim Philby at a pre-war dinner held by the Anglo-German Fellowship, reproduced in *The Philby Conspiracy* by Bruce Page and Philip Knightley, appears to have been retouched.

But the details which seem to have got most mixed up are those concerning the assassination of Reinhard Heydrich, the Reich Protector of Bohemia Moldavia, for the author seems to think the two assassins were trained in Canada and that Sir William Stephenson himself was involved in this episode of the war.

There were, in fact, originally two plans to assassinate a senior Nazi official. The first, from Major Vaclav Moravek, identified Karl Frank as the target. Moravek was one of the original leaders of the Czech resistance movement, UVOD, and had remained in his homeland after the German occupation. Frank was a Sudeten German and Secretary of State in the Protectorate's government. Moravek 'had transmitted the idea to General Bartik (the Director of Czech Military Intelligence in London) as early as September 1939'.[9]

In an account written by the head of the Czech government-in-exile's Deuxième Bureau, Frantisek Moravec, the idea was pursued 'late in 1941'[10] by President Beneš. He recalls: 'In the discussions of the President's idea, two potential targets for assassination appeared suitable. One of them was the Czech quisling, Emanuel Moravec . . . the other was Heydrich himself.' Moravec describes how he imposed very strict security on the plan: 'the only people in London to know the whole plan would be, in addition to the President and myself, my deputy, Lieutenant-Colonel Strankmueller, and one of my staff officers, Captain Fryc'.[11] The number of people authorized to know about the plan was so limited that the senior Czech officer in England and the Minister of National Defence, 'General Ingr, who knew all about our special missions . . . did not know the mission's purpose'.

In spite of this tight security there was, Moravec concedes, an operational requirement to consult with the British and collaborate over certain technical aspects of the mission. Moravec explains: 'This knowledge was necessarily shared with several officials of the British MI6, who worked with us on the technical side of this as well as all the other special operations.'

Josef Gabcik and Jan Kubis were the two originally chosen to carry out the assassination and both came from the same refugee camp in Poland when war broke out in September 1940. They had escaped from German-occupied Czechoslovakia and were anxious to fight the Nazis. Accordingly they both joined the French Foreign Legion and fought on the Western Front in May and June 1940. When the Legionnaires were evacuated to England they volunteered for the 1st Czech Brigade, then based at Cholmondeley Castle, near Whitchurch in Cheshire. Here they were issued with British army paybooks: Gabcik with No 1221, Kubis with No 1273.

It was not until April 1941 that the British War Office gave its consent for a total of nine Czechs (four officers and five NCOs) to begin a parachute training course at SOE's Special Training School at Ringway, outside Manchester. From an official Czech government-in-exile document dated 19 May 1941 comes further details concerning the personnel selected to attend the course at

Ringway. Apparently Moravec had succeeded in increasing the number of candidates to thirty-six, each of whom was to undergo the three-week programme. The thirty-sixth name on the list of men provided by the CO of the Czech 1st Brigade is that of Josef Gabcik.

Gabcik completed the course at Ringway and returned to Cholmondeley Castle at the end of June 1941. Thereafter he went to SOE's school of sabotage at Cammus Durrah, near Mallaig in the Scottish highlands, and, after a further spell at Cholmondeley, he was assigned to Bellasis, a country house near Dorking used by SOE as a staging area for agents about to go into occupied territory. On 3 October 1941 Gabcik attended a conference in London with Moravec and his intended partner, Sergeant Svoboda. They were informed of their target, the Reich protector Heydrich, and asked whether they wished to withdraw. Both agreed to go, and the operation was set to begin exactly a week later. The actual date of the assassination was scheduled for the Czech National Holiday, 28 October.

As it turned out the weather on the appointed day was atrocious and the operation was called off. Subsequent attempts on 7 and 30 November were also cancelled because snow storms obscured the dropping zones. The two assassins spent the intervening period undergoing further training, and in one exercise Svoboda sustained an injury that prevented him from participating further. His replacement was Jan Kubis, who had been through the same training programme. In the weeks before their final trip to Tangmere, Gabcik and Kubis were befriended by two teenage girls, Lorna and Edna Ellison, who lived at Ightfield, some four miles from Cholmondeley. As a result both men spent most of their spare time and their weekends staying with the Ellison family at their small, two-storey home. There is absolutely no evidence that either Gabcik or Kubis ever went to Canada, and the evidence of their attendance at various SOE training schools confirms that there could not have been time for them to visit Camp X in Canada between Gabcik's acceptance on the parachute course at Ringway in June 1941 (which lasted three weeks) and his minuted presence at Moravec's conference in London on 3 October. In the intervening time he is known to have been at Inverness-shire and Cholmondeley Castle.

It would not have been possible for Gabcik and Kubis to have fitted an Atlantic crossing into their tight schedule so it is unlikely that they ever encountered William Stephenson of BSC in New York.

It also seems equally unlikely that the SOE agent Noor Inayat Khan, code-named MADELEINE, ever met William Stephenson 'during one of her family journeys back to India in 1934' or 'in a tiger shoot', as in 1934 MADELEINE was a student at the Ecole Normale de Musique de Paris and had spent her vacation touring Spain. In fact, she only visited India once in her life, in the autumn of 1928, when she went on a family pilgrimage to visit her father's grave. At the time she was fifteen years old. Neither her brother nor her sister, who both accompanied her, can recall participating in a tiger hunt. Both insist the incident is a fantasy and point out that a political discussion between a fifteen-year-old girl and a successful industrialist is scarcely likely.

Nor was MADELEINE recruited by William Stephenson. Noor Inayat Khan joined the Women's Auxiliary Air Force on 19 November 1940. She did so because her younger brother Vilayat had recently joined the RAF. It seems unlikely that anyone was taking an interest in her recruitment. When she first tried to join up her application was refused on the grounds that she was not a British subject. She then had to write to the officer in charge of the recruiting office, who confirmed that a British Protected Person was indeed eligible to join the WAAFs, and processed her application. Her transfer to SOE took place in October 1942 (and not in April, as suggested by Stevenson) after she had completed her training as a WAAF radio operator. The Commissions Board had turned down her application for a commission, but because of her knowledge of French she had been recommended for a job in Intelligence. She was therefore interviewed by Selwyn Jepson and taken on for training as an agent and wireless operator. According to both Selwyn Jepson and Vera Atkins (who, incidentally, was never MADELEINE's 'CO, or Conducting Officer'[12]) Stephenson played no part whatever in MADELEINE's recruitment.

When MADELEINE's friend and biographer, Jean Overton Fuller, first read *A Man Called Intrepid*, she was mystified by the author's concentration on MADELEINE's story. When she reread it, she noticed a large number of references that could only have come from her own book, which had been published by Gollancz in 1952. When Miss Fuller came to compare Stevenson's account with her own, she noticed dozens of similarities. For example, on page 338 Stevenson says: 'Jepson agreed to let her start training, "with rather more of the bleak distress which I never failed to feel at this point in these interviews".' Stevenson's use of the quotation marks implies that Jepson spoke those words to the author. He didn't. But Jepson did contribute a section of his recollections to Miss Fuller's book. On page 111 Jepson recalls that Noor Inayat Khan '"would like to try to become an agent for us, if I thought she could make it. I had not the slightest doubt that she could, and said so, and with rather more of the bleak distress which I never failed to feel at this point I agreed to take her on."' Miss

Fuller found various other pieces of information which could only have come from her research. She also spotted that Stevenson had been so faithful in his version that he had even copied her spelling mistakes!

Miss Fuller contacted Stevenson's British publisher, Macmillans, and presented them with her evidence. They promptly agreed to delete all references to MADELEINE in the English paperback editions, although these alterations were not subsequently made in the American editions.

My special interest has been the British Security Service, MI5, and I have, over the years, made a study of its operations. Several small details concerning the organization are askew in *A Man Called Intrepid*. For instance, George Johnson Armstrong, the first Briton of the war to be hanged for treachery, is listed in the index as George R. Armstrong and in the text is referred to as George Thomas Armstrong.

Armstrong was arrested in Boston by the American authorities after he had been spotted offering his services as a spy to a German diplomat. He was taken into custody, then deported to Britain on board the SS *La Brea* for his journey across the Atlantic, and he was kept in leg irons for the duration of the passage. The ship docked at Cardiff in Wales, where he was met by Detective Inspector Louden Roberts of the Cardiff City Police. He was hanged on 10 July 1941.

Unfortunately *A Man Called Intrepid* has this slightly wrong as it says that Armstrong sailed back to England, where Scotland Yard picked him up, and that he was hanged on 9 July 1941. Again small points, but if these are later accepted as true and used to prove some other information as correct then history will become muddled.

Errors, slips and tangles are inevitable in describing a world of secret activity in which the officials involved are sworn to silence. But as the war recedes in time, enough documents are now coming to light to enable some facts to be firmly established. A great many bizarre and unorthodox activities occurred during wartime which are fascinating to read about and to uncover. Often the correct version is even more extraordinary than the garbled one and even more revealing about the people involved. Certainly this is true of Sir William Stephenson, whose unique career was quite remarkable enough and never needed any embroidery or exaggeration to enhance it.

Postscript: Another Intrepid?

Nothing deceives like a document.
> WILLIAM STEVENSON quoting Sir William
> Stephenson in *The Bormann Brotherhood*

Will wartime intelligence mythology continue as a growth industry? All the indications point that way, and in recent years there has been a perceptible increase in the number of people claiming either to have participated in previously unknown organizations or operations, or simply to have discovered some breathtaking exploit which had previously remained a secret.

An example of the former can be found in the intriguing autobiography *Churchill's Secret Agent*, which purported to relate the authentic non-fiction wartime experiences of Dr Josephine Butler, who had been

recruited by Winston Churchill as the only woman member of his élite 'Secret Circle'. Its existence unsuspected by even the War Office or MI5, the 'Secret Circle' was Churchill's closest ring of intelligence agents, answerable only to him, and instrumental in obtaining the information necessary for the successful liberation of Europe. None of the twelve members ever knew the identity of the others.

Dr Butler explains that the Prime Minister did not want to involve his own wartime staff, for her activities were too secret even for them. She then claims to have flown over fifty missions into enemy territory from RAF Tempsford in Lysanders.

However, none of her alleged flights from RAF Tempsford have been recorded and she makes enough mistakes about Lysander aircraft to confirm that she had probably never been near one. In addition, the Secret Intelligence Service liaison officer stationed at Tempsford during the relevant period, Bruce Bonsey, has flatly denied her story. However secret an operation, the flight would have to have been cleared through him, and he cannot recall a single one, let alone a record fifty, by the same agent.

Dr Butler's story appeared to be a work of fiction but the fact that she was published under a non-fiction listing means that someone, somewhere, was fooled. In fact, she had relied upon half-a-dozen identifiable books relating the adventures of agents in occupied France. Using these as a foundation she had woven her own plausible fantasy. Such inventions often rely on the alleged participation of individuals who have long since died, thus making evidence all the harder to obtain. Very occasionally, a mythologist blunders and assumes a person to be beyond the grave when he is, in fact, available to expose a fabrication. In late 1983 just such an event took place.

In *Intrepid's Last Case* William Stevenson returns to the subject of his previous *oeuvre*, Sir William Stephenson, and creates a sequel based on the defection in September 1945 of a young cipher clerk from the Soviet Embassy in Ottawa. The defection of Igor Gouzenko really took place, and Sir William had flown up to Canada from New York (where his job as Director of British Security Co-ordination had come to an end) and persuaded the Canadian authorities to offer the defector asylum. If he had not done so, there is every chance that Gouzenko would have been handed back to the Soviets, along with the secret dossiers that he had purloined from the Soviet Embassy. Documents from these files identified a number of Soviet agents in North America and resulted in, among others, the arrest and conviction of atomic physicist Allan Nunn May, code-named ALEK, the following year.

In his book Stevenson says that he had special access to reports classified as top secret and the 'previously embargoed BSC file on Gouzenko's case'.

Making use of these files Stevenson records Nunn May's first interrogation by MI5's William Skardon, which, he suggests, took place 'at May's lodgings near the University of London on February 14'. Stevenson reproduces the conversation that followed verbatim, and describes how 'After four visits Skardon had started to trip up the scientist.'[1]

Eventually the brilliant interrogator had broken through the wall of evasion:

Skardon had delivered his customary little lecture to Professor May on the advisability of co-operating with the authorities. If a spy confessed fully and frankly, life would be made tolerable. In some cases, where no confession was volunteered, the spy would be promised immunity from prosecution. In May's case the co-operation was strictly limited.

Stevenson also gave a description of Skardon's remarkable background: 'Skardon had developed his style during wartime interrogation of Nazis and captured German commanders. U-boat captains, in particular, were disarmed by the man's concern to offer no discourtesy.'[2]

However, apparently unknown to Stevenson, Skardon is alive and well, and living in quiet retirement on the south coast of England. He told me that he has never met a U-boat commander in his life and he never interrogated Allan Nunn May. He did, however, meet Nunn May briefly after his release from prison, on an entirely different matter (a corrupt journalist, as it happens).

In fact, the first interrogation of Professor Nunn May was conducted by Leonard Burt and Reginald Spooner.

After his retirement Len Burt, in *Commander Burt of the Yard*, published in 1959, wrote:

> The great strength of our position was that we were both officers of the Intelligence Corps, Lieutenant-Colonel Burt and Major Spooner, both in uniform. These were the men whom the man we believed to be Alek found himself confronted with when the atomic energy authorities asked him to call at Shell-Mex House on 15 February 1946.[3]

Thus, according to Burt, Stevenson's version had miscast the main players and been wrong over both the date and location of the fateful meeting. Later, Reg Spooner's biographer, Iain Adamson, confirmed these details in 1966 in *The Great Detective*, where he makes it clear that Allan Nunn May kept his appointment 'with Burt and Spooner in an office in Shell-Mex House on February 15, 1946'.[4]

Evidently these accounts had missed Stevenson's attention, and so, apparently, had Skardon's own version of the Nunn May interrogation. Although few people had been in on the secret, Skardon had dictated details of the Nunn May case direct from MI5's files to Alan Moorehead in 1952. He had been instructed to do so by the then Director-General of the Security Service, Sir Percy Sillitoe, in a unique bid to counter recent bad publicity. In *The Traitors*, published in 1952, Moorehead wrote, at Skardon's direction: 'In London, May was for the first time interrogated directly. Commander Burt saw him at Shell-Mex House.'[5]

Stevenson's version was an imaginary one, but to readers it suggests that the legendary Skardon persuaded Allan Nunn May to crack. Paradoxically, it is a myth on which Skardon has exercised a negative influence.

The occasional mistake or typographical error will slip past the notice of the most diligent author or editor.

However eminent the historian, there will always be honest mistakes. But some authors become over-enthusiastic and allow their imaginations excessively free rein. The combination of fantasy and fact is very readable and extremely popular but – unchecked – it has the effect of rewriting history. Once a controversy has been initiated erroneously, the mud tends to stick. Once President Roosevelt is suspected of having had forewarning about Japanese intentions to bomb Pearl Harbor, the allegation will gain credence each time it is repeated until someone bothers to disprove the story. If the myth gains currency, it may establish itself permanently and even become accepted as a historical fact. What makes the intelligence world so susceptible to the syndrome is the traditional, but entirely understandable, reluctance of former (or, for that matter, current) intelligence officers and agents to 'go public' and nail a lie. In consequence an author can invent a non-existent spy and have his book categorized as a serious work of historical non-fiction, safe in the knowledge that the odds are against an official contradiction.

This book has tried to show how legends develop around genuine events. Where an operation has gone badly wrong, those taking part feel betrayed. People start to look for scapegoats and, in the tangled world of espionage, it is easy to speculate about who might have been guilty of an act of treachery. All too soon the speculation becomes accepted.

There is a world of difference between the peddling of a relatively harmless legend, like that of Albert Oertel and the sinking of HMS *Royal Oak*, and the more sinister accusation that Winston Churchill sat by idly while the Luftwaffe planned to flatten Coventry. Neither can the differing interpretations of CICERO's activities be classified as being in the same league as the serious allegations made against certain double agents in the destruction of the RAF's raid on Nuremberg. Nevertheless, the agents have a right to reply.

This book could only have been written with the help and guidance of some of those intelligence officers and their agents who participated in secret wartime operations. A few, such as Roman Garby-Czerniawski, have already written their memoirs and realize they will not be offered two bites of the cherry. Others, like Dusko Popov, have actually contributed to the development of a myth by only being able to tell one side of a story. All TATE wishes to do is live the rest of his life in quiet retirement without having to listen to ill-founded accusations that he betrayed the Dieppe raid and conspired to kill hundreds of Allied troops. If the reputation of one person can be saved by this book, be he a relatively small cog, like TATE, or be he a big wheel, such as Churchill, it will have achieved its purpose.

Notes

Introduction

1 M. R. D. Foot, *MI9*, p. 80
2 Henry Landau, *All's Fair*, p. 206
3 Ladislas Farago, *Game of the Foxes*, p. 281
4 Charles Wighton and Gunter Peis, *Hitler's Spies and Saboteurs*, p. 245
5 Gilles Perrault, *The Secrets of D-Day*, p. 32
6 Stanley Firmin, *They Came to Spy*, p. 50
7 *Ibid.*, p. 49
8 Jock Haswell, *The Intelligence and Deception of the D-Day Landings*, p. 61
9 *Ibid.*, p. 62
10 Bernard Newman, *Spies in Britain*, p. 57
11 Bernard Newman, *Spy Catchers*, p. 38
12 Haswell, *op. cit.*, p. 58

1 MOONLIGHT SONATA or Sacrifice?

1 Brian Johnson, *The Secret War*, p. 48
2 F. W. Winterbotham, *The Ultra Secret*, p. 60
3 *Ibid.*, p. 61
4 Anthony Cave Brown, *Bodyguard of Lies*, p. 40
5 *Ibid.*, p. 41
6 *Ibid.*, p. 42
7 William Stevenson, *A Man Called Intrepid*, p. 165 (all extracts reproduced by kind permission of Macmillan, London and Basingstoke)
8 *Ibid.*

9 *Ibid.*
10 See Aileen Clayton, *The Enemy is Listening*, p. 82
11 See A. V. Jones, *Most Secret War*, p. 139
12 PRO AIR 2/5238
13 See F. H. Hinsley, *British Intelligence in the Second World War*, Vol. 1, p. 318

2 Canaris: Traitor or Hero?

1 Kurt Singer, *Spies and Traitors of World War II*, p. 4
2 *Ibid.*, p. 6
3 Major Thomas Coulson, *Mata Hari: Courtesan and Spy*, p. 172
4 Arch Whitehouse, *Espionage and Counterespionage*, p. 59
5 Sir Basil Thomson, *Queer People*, p. 184
6 *Ibid.*, p. 182
7 Richard Rowan, *Spy and Counter-Spy*, p. 292
8 Hugh Cleland Hoy, *40 O.B.*, p. 156
9 Admiral Sir William James, *The Eyes of the Navy*, p. 36
10 Richard Deacon, *A History of the British Secret Service*, p. 273
11 Robert Goldston, *Sinister Touches: The Secret War Against Hitler*, p. 104
12 Cave Brown, *Bodyguard of Lies*, p. 143
13 *Ibid.*, p. 144
14 Bodo Herzog, *Die Nachhut*, 8 January 1973, p. 43
15 David Kahn, *Hitler's Spies*, p. 227
16 Cave Brown, *op. cit.*, p. 154
17 Ian Colvin, *Canaris: Chief of Intelligence*, p. 5
18 George Constantinides, *Intelligence and Espionage: An Analytical Bibliography*, p. 132
19 Herbert Molloy Mason, *To Kill The Devil*, p. 44
20 Ian Colvin, *Canaris: Hitler's Secret Enemy*, p. 8

21 F. W. Winterbotham, *Secret and Personal*, p. 162
22 Deacon, *op. cit.*, p. 283
23 André Brissaud, *Canaris*, p. 273
24 *Ibid.*, p. xiv
25 *Ibid.*, p. xv
26 Heinz Höhne, *Canaris*, p. 485
27 *Ibid.*, p. 486
28 Anthony Cave Brown, *The Last Hero*, p. 129
29 *Ibid.*, p. 758
30 *Ibid.*
31 *Ibid.*, p. 293
32 Richard Dunlop, *America's Master Spy*, p. 4
33 Paul Leverkühn, *German Military Intelligence*, p. 206
34 Kahn, *op. cit.*, p. 235
35 Pierre Galante, *Operation Valkyrie*, p. 69
36 *Ibid.*, p. 163
37 Hans von Herwarth, *Against Two Evils*, p. 268
38 Colvin, *Canaris: Chief of Intelligence*, p. 89
39 *Ibid.*, p. 90
40 *Ibid.*, p. 92
41 *Sunday Times*, 16 October 1983

3 The Agent from Orkney

1 William Shirer, *Berlin Diary*, p. 190
2 Alexandre Korganoff, *The Phantom of Scapa Flow*, p. 183
3 PRO ADM 199/158
4 Singer, *Spies and Traitors of World War II*, p. v
5 *Ibid.*, p. 84
6 *Ibid.*, p. 61
7 *Ibid.*, p. 63
8 *Ibid.*, p. 87
9 *Ibid.*, p. 86
10 *Ibid.*, p. 82

11 Kurt Singer, *More Spy Stories*, p. 60
12 E. H. Cookridge, *Secrets of the British Secret Service*, p. 63
13 *Ibid.*, p. 65
14 *Ibid.*, p. 66
15 *Ibid.*, p. 67
16 *Ibid.*,
17 *Ibid.*, p. 66
18 *Ibid.*, p. vi
19 Walter Schellenberg, *The Labyrinth*, p. 9
20 *Ibid.*, p. 14
21 *Ibid.*, p. 62
22 John Bulloch, *MI5*, p. 170
23 Farago, *Game of the Foxes*, p. 188
24 Christopher Felix, *The Spy and his Masters: A Short Course in the Secret War*, p. 123
25 E. H. Cookridge, *The Third Man*, p. 101
26 Geoffrey Cousins, *The Story of Scapa Flow*, p. 147
27 Letter to author, 3 November 1983
28 Richard Deacon, *The Silent War*, p. 152
29 Conversation with author, 29 March 1984

4 Who Was WERTHER?

1 Allen Dulles, *The Craft of Intelligence*, p. 111
2 Pierre Accoce and Pierre Quet, *The Lucy Ring*, p. 58 (all extracts © Librairie Academique Perrin 1966; English language translation © W. H. Allen & Co. and Coward-McCann Inc. 1967)
3 *Ibid.*, p. 70
4 *Ibid.*, p. 71
5 *Ibid.*, p. 72
6 *Ibid.*, p. 73
7 *Ibid.*, p. 74
8 Alexander Rado, *Codename Dora*, p. xxi (all extracts

reproduced by kind permission of Blackie and Son Ltd)

9 *Ibid.*, p. 295

10 See Gert Buchheit, *Die deutsche Geheimdienst* (List Verlag, 1966) and Wilhelm von Schramm, 'Die rot-weisse Kapelle', *Frankfurter Allgemeine Zeitung*, 13 December 1966

11 Rado, *op. cit.*, p. 137

12 *Ibid.*, p. 136

13 *Ibid.*, p. 141

14 *Ibid.*

15 *Ibid.*, p. 137

16 *Ibid.*, p. 136

17 *Ibid.*, p. 139

18 Paul Kesaris (ed.), *The Rote Kapelle*, p. 224

19 *Ibid.*, p. 332

20 Anthony Read and David Fisher, *Operation Lucy*, p. 88

21 *Ibid.*, p. 98

22 *Ibid.*, p. 146

23 *Ibid.*, p. 147

24 Kesaris, *op. cit.*, p. 214

25 Read and Fisher, *op. cit.*, p. 219

26 Rado, *op. cit.*, p. 145

27 Letter to author, 18 February 1983

28 Professor Garlinski, *The Swiss Corridor*, p. 83

29 Rado, *op. cit.*, p. 146

30 Kesaris, *op. cit.*, p. 185

31 *Ibid.*, p. 192

32 *Ibid.*, p. 178

5 Pearl Harbor: A Warning Ignored?

1 Sir John Masterman, *The Double Cross System in the War of 1939–1945*, p. 80

2 *Ibid.*
3 Dusko Popov, *Spy Counterspy*, p. 116
4 Masterman, *op. cit.*, p. 79
5 Popov, *op. cit.*, p. 122
6 *Ibid.*, p. 123
7 *Ibid.*, p. 124
8 John Toland, *Infamy*, p. 366 (all extracts reproduced by kind permission of Methuen & Co. Ltd.)
9 *Ibid.*, p. 15
10 *Ibid.*, p. 269
11 Commander Philip Johns, *Within Two Cloaks*, p. 60
12 Popov, *op. cit.*, p. 132
13 Donald Whitehead, *The FBI Story*, p. 196
14 Toland, *op. cit.*, p. 271n
15 Letter to *The Times*, 5 September 1982
16 Toland, *op. cit.*, p. 118
17 *Ibid.*, p. 119

6 JUBILEE or Betrayal?

1 Terence Robertson, *Dieppe*, pp. 402–3
2 James Leasor, *Green Beach*, p. 101
3 Robertson, *op. cit.*, p. 206
4 *Ibid.*, p. 387
5 Stanley Lovell, *Of Spies and Stratagems*, p. 153
6 *Ibid.*, p. 154
7 Masterman, *The Double Cross System . . .* , p. 108
8 Gunter Peis, *The Mirror of Deception*, p. 122
9 *Ibid.*, p. 123
10 *Ibid.*, p. 124
11 Leonard Mosley, *The Druid*, p. 116
12 *Ibid.*, p. 104
13 *Ibid.*, p. 16
14 *Ibid.*, p. 17
15 *Ibid.*, p. 43

16 *Ibid.*, p. 76
17 *Ibid.*, p. 118
18 Mosley, *op. cit.*, p. 97
19 Lovell, *op. cit.*, p. 157
20 Hinsley, *British Intelligence in the Second World War*, Vol. 1, p. 695
21 Masterman, *op. cit.*, p. 108
22 Hinsley, *op. cit.*, p. 697
23 *Ibid.*, p. 702

7 CICERO: A Stratagem of Deception?

1 Dulles, *The Craft of Intelligence*, p. 153
2 Allen Dulles, *The Secret Surrender*, p. 24
3 Kermit Roosevelt, *The War Report of the OSS*, p. 278
4 Ludwig Moyzisch, *Operation Cicero*, p. 129
5 *Ibid.*, p. 44
6 *Ibid.*, p. 81
7 Schellenberg, *The Labyrinth*, p. 392
8 Letter to the *Daily Telegraph*, 26 April 1971
9 Cave Brown, *Bodyguard of Lies*, p. 399
10 *Ibid.*, p. 400
11 *Ibid.*, p. 402
12 *Ibid.*, p. 403
13 Constantine FitzGibbon, *Secret Intelligence in the Twentieth Century*, p. 261
14 *Ibid.*, p. 263
15 Sir Fitzroy Maclean, *Take Nine Steps*, p. 221

8 KING KONG of Arnhem

1 Peer de Silva, *Sub Rosa: The CIA and the Uses of Intelligence*, p. 79
2 Oreste Pinto, *Spycatcher*, p. 111
3 *Ibid.*, p. 127

4 *Ibid.*, p. 139
5 *Ibid.*, p. 142
6 Hermann Giskes, *London Calling North Pole*, p. 171
7 *Ibid.*, p. 172
8 Anne Laurens, *The Lindemans Affair*, p. 119
9 *Ibid.*, p. 134
10 Pinto, *op. cit.*, p. 122
11 *Ibid.*, p. 144
12 *Ibid.*, p. 145
13 Laurens, *op. cit.*, p. 169
14 *Ibid.*
15 Pinto, *op. cit.*, p. 135
16 Laurens, *op. cit.*, p. 183
17 *Ibid.*, p. 170
18 *Ibid.*, p. 183
19 *Ibid.*, p. 146
20 John Bulloch, *Akin to Treason*, p. 101
21 Colonel J. M. Langley, *Fight Another Day*, p. 227
22 *Ibid.*, p. 288
23 *Ibid.*, p. 229

9 Nuremberg: The Double Cross

1 Hinsley, *British Intelligence in the Second World War*, Vol. III, p. 566
2 Cave Brown, *Bodyguard of Lies*, p. 151
3 Masterman, *The Double Cross System . . .* , p. 9
4 *Ibid.*, p. 148
5 *Ibid.*
6 Jones, *Most Secret War*, p. 393

10 A Man Called *Intrepid?*

1 Stevenson, *A Man Called Intrepid*, p. xiv
2 *Ibid.*, p. xix

3 *Ibid.*, p. 112
4 *Ibid.*, p. 92
5 See Hinsley, *British Intelligence in the Second World War*, Vol. I, p. 139
6 *Ibid.*, p. 163
7 Stevenson, *op. cit.*, p. 141
8 Hinsley, *op. cit.*, p. 108
9 Jan Weiner, *The Assassination of Heydrich*, p. 42
10 Frantisec Moravec, *Master of Spies*, p. 210
11 *Ibid.*, p. 211
12 Stevenson, *op. cit.*, p. 243

Postscript: Another *Intrepid?*

1 William Stevenson, *Intrepid's Last Case*, p. 162
2 *Ibid.*, p. 161
3 Leonard Burt, *Commander Burt of the Yard*, p. 36
4 Iain Adamson, *The Great Detective*, p. 155
5 Alan Moorehead, *The Traitors*, p. 36

Bibliography

Abshagen, Karl Heinz, *Canaris* (Hutchinson, 1956; Union Deutsche Verlagsgesellschaft, 1949)

Accoce, Pierre, and Quet, Pierre, *The Lucy Ring* (W. H. Allen, 1967; as *A Man Called Lucy*, Coward-McCann, 1967)

Adamson, Iain, *The Great Detective* (Muller, 1966)

Bancroft, Mary, *Autobiography of a Spy* (Morrow, 1983)

Bazna, Elyesa, *I Was Cicero* (Andre Deutsche, 1962; Collins, Ontario, 1962)

Beevor, J. G., *SOE Reflections* (Bodley Head, 1981)

Boucherdon, Pierre, *Souvenirs* (Albin Michel, Paris, 1953)

Boveri, Margaret, *Treason in the Twentieth Century* (Putnams, 1978)

Brissaud, André, *Canaris* (Weidenfeld & Nicolson, 1973; Grosset, 1974)

Buckmaster, Maurice, *We Fought Alone* (Odhams, 1958; W. W. Norton, 1959)

Bulloch, John, *MI5* (Arthur Barker, 1963)

Bulloch, John, *Akin to Treason* (Arthur Barker, 1966)

Burgess, Alan, *Seven Men at Daybreak* (Evans, 1960; Dutton, 1960)

Burt, Leonard, *Commander Burt of the Yard* (Heinemann, 1959)

Büsch, Harald, *U-Boats at War* (Putnam, 1955)

Butler, Josephine, *Churchill's Secret Agent* (Blaketon-Hall, 1983)

Calvocoressi, Peter, *Top Secret Ultra* (Cassells, 1980; Pantheon Books, 1980)

Cave Brown, Anthony, *Bodyguard of Lies* (W. H. Allen, 1976; Harper & Row, 1975)

Cave Brown, Anthony, *The Last Hero* (Times, 1982; Michael Joseph, 1983)

Churchill, Sir Winston, *The Gathering Storm* (Cassells, 1948; Houghton Mifflin, 1951)

Clark, Ronald, *The Man Who Broke Purple* (Weidenfeld & Nicolson, 1977; Little, Brown, 1977)

Clarke, Dudley, *Seven Assignments* (Cape, 1948; Clarke, Irwin, 1948)

Clayton, Aileen, *The Enemy is Listening* (Hutchinson, 1980; Ballantine Books, 1982)

Collier, Basil, *Hidden Weapons* (Hamish Hamilton, 1982; David & Charles, New York, 1982)

Colvin, Ian, *Chief of Intelligence* (Gollancz, 1951; as *Master Spy*, McGraw Hill, 1951; as *Hitler's Secret Enemy*, Pan, 1957)

Constantinides, George, *Intelligence and Espionage: An Analytical Bibliography* (Westview Press, 1983)

Cookridge, E. H. (pseud. of Edward Spiro), *Secrets of the British Secret Service* (Low, Marston, 1947)

Cookridge, E. H., *They Came From The Sky* (Heinemann, 1965; Crowell, 1967)

Cookridge, E. H., *Inside S.O.E.* (Arthur Barker, 1966; as *Set Europe Ablaze*, Crowell, 1967)

Cookridge, E. H., *The Third Man* (Arthur Barker, 1968; Putnam, 1968)

Costello, John, *The Pacific War* (Rawson, Wade, 1981)

Coulson, Thomas, *Mata Hari: Courtesan and Spy* (Hutchinson, 1930; Harper, 1930)

Cousins, Geoffrey, *The Story of Scapa Flow* (Muller, 1965)

Cruickshank, Charles, *Deception in World War II* (OUP, London, 1979; OUP, New York, 1980)

Dallin, David, *Soviet Espionage* (OUP, 1956; Yale, 1955)

Davidson, Basil, *Special Operations Europe* (Gollancz, 1980)

Deacon, Richard (pseud. of Donald McCormick), *A History of the British Secret Service* (Muller, 1969; Taplinger, 1970)

Deacon, Richard, *A History of the Russian Secret Service* (Muller, 1972; Taplinger, 1972)

Deacon, Richard, *The Silent War* (David & Charles, 1978; Hippocrene Books, 1978)

Deacon, Richard, *The British Connection* (Hamish Hamilton, 1979)

Delmer, Sefton, *The Counterfeit Spy* (Hutchinson, 1973)

Deschner, Günther, *Heydrich* (Orbis, 1982; Stein & Day, 1981)

De Silva, Peer, *Sub Rosa: The CIA and the Uses of Intelligence* (Times, 1978)

Dodds-Parker, Sir Douglas, *Setting Europe Ablaze* (Springwood, 1983)

Doenitz, Karl, *Memoirs* (Weidenfeld & Nicolson, 1959; World Publishers, N.Y., 1959)

Dulles, Allen W., *Germany's Underground* (Macmillan, 1947)

Dulles, Allen W., *The Craft of Intelligence* (Weidenfeld & Nicolson, 1964; Harper & Row, 1963)

Dulles, Allen W., *The Secret Surrender* (Weidenfeld & Nicolson, 1967; Harper & Row, 1966)

Dulles, Allen W., *Great True Spy Stories* (Collins, 1969; Harper & Row, 1968)

Dunlop, Richard, *America's Master Spy* (Rand McNally, 1982)

Ellis, C. H., *The Transcaspian Episode* (Hutchinson, 1963)

Farago, Ladislas, *Burn after Reading* (Walker, 1961)

Farago, Ladislas, *The Broken Seal* (Arthur Barker, 1967; Random House, 1967)

Farago, Ladislas, *Game of the Foxes* (Hodder & Stoughton, 1972; McKay, 1971)

Felix, Christopher (pseud. of James MacCargar), *The Spy and his Masters: A Short Course in the Secret War* (Secker & Warburg, 1963; Clarke, Irwin, 1962)

Firmin, Stanley, *They Came to Spy* (Hutchinson, 1950; Ryerson Press, Toronto, 1951)

FitzGibbon, Constantine, *To Kill Hitler* (Tom Stacey, 1972; originally published as *The Shirt of Nessus*, Cassells, 1956; Norton, N.Y., 1956)

FitzGibbon, Constantine, *Secret Intelligence in the Twentieth Century* (Hart-Davis MacGibbon, 1976; Stein & Day, 1976)

Foot, M. R. D., *SOE in France* (HMSO, 1966)

Foot, M. R. D., and Langley, J. M., *MI9* (Bodley Head, 1979; Little, Brown, 1980)

Foote, Alexander, *Handbook for Spies* (Museum Press, 1949; Doubleday, 1949)

Frank, Wolfgang, *Enemy Submarine* (William Kimber, 1954)

Frischauer, Willi, *The Man Who Came Back* (Muller, 1958; S. J. R. Saunders, Toronto, 1958)

Fuller, Jean Overton, *Madeleine* (Gollancz, 1952; Bond Street Publishers, Toronto, 1952)

Fuller, Jean Overton, *The Starr Affair* (Gollancz, 1954; as *No. 13, Bob*, Little, Brown, 1955)

Fuller, Jean Overton, *Double Webs* (Putnam, 1955)

Fuller, Jean Overton, *The German Penetration of SOE* (William Kimber, 1975)

Galante, Pierre, *Operation Valkyrie* (Harper & Row, 1981)

Gallagher, Matthew, *The Soviet History of World War II* (Praeger, London & New York, 1963)

Garby-Czerniawski, *The Big Network* (George Ronald, 1961; Copp Clarke, Toronto, 1961)

Garlinski, Josef, *Intercept: The Enigma War* (Dent, 1980; as *The Enigma War*, Scribner, 1980)

Garlinski, Josef, *The Swiss Corridor* (J. M. Dent, 1981)

Gisevius, Hans Bernd, *To the Bitter End* (Cape, 1948; Houghton Mifflin, 1947)

Giskes, Hermann, *London Calling North Pole* (William Kimber, 1953)

Goldston, Richard, *Sinister Touches: The Secret War Against Hitler* (Dial Press, 1982)

Gordon, Harold, *Hitler and the Beer Hall Putsch* (Princeton, 1972)

Haswell, Jock, *British Military Intelligence* (Weidenfeld & Nicolson, 1973)

Haswell, Jock, *The Intelligence and Deception of the D-Day Landings* (Batsford, 1979; as *D-Day: Intelligence and Deception*, Times, 1980)

Herwath, Hans von, *Against Two Evils* (Collins, 1981; Rawson Wade, 1981)

Herzog, Bodo, 'Canaris', *Die Nachhut*, January 1973

Hinsley, F. H., *British Intelligence in the Second World War*, Vols II & III (HMSO, 1979, 1981 and 1984; Cambridge University Press, N.Y., 1979)

Hoehling, A. A., *Women Who Spied* (Dodd, Mead, 1967)

Hoffmann, Peter, *The History of the German Resistance 1933–1945* (Macdonald & Jane's, 1972)

Höhne, Heinz, *Canaris* (Secker & Warburg, 1979; Doubleday, 1979)

Höhne, Heinz, *Codeword: Direktor* (Secker & Warburg, 1971)

Holmes, W. J., *Double-Edged Secrets* (Naval Institute Press, 1979)

Hoover, J. Edgar, *The Masterpiece of Espionage* (Reader's Digest, 1964)

Hoy, Hugh Cleland, *40 O.B.* (Hutchinson, 1932)

Hutton, J. Bernard, *Women Spies* (W.H. Allen, 1972; as *Women in Espionage*, Macmillan, 1971)

Hyde, H.M., *The Quiet Canadian* (Hamish Hamilton, 1962; as *Room 3603*, Farrar, Straus, 1963)

Hyde, H.M., *Cynthia* (Hamish Hamilton, 1966; Farrar, Straus, 1965)

Hyde, H.M., *The Atom Bomb Spies* (Hamish Hamilton, 1980; Atheneum, 1980)

Hyde, H.M., *Secret Intelligence Agent* (Constable, 1982; St Martin's Press, 1983)

Ind, Allison, *A History of Modern Espionage* (Hodder & Stoughton, 1965; McKay, 1963)

Ivanov, Miroslav, *The Assassination of Heydrich* (Hart-Davis, 1973; as *Target: Heydrich*, Macmillan, N.Y., 1974)

Jackson, Robert, *The Secret Squadrons* (Robson, 1983; Hippocrene Books, 1983)

James, Sir William, *The Eyes of the Navy* (Methuen, 1955; as *Code Breakers of Room 40*, St Martin's Press, 1956)

John, Otto, *Twice Through the Lines* (Macmillan, 1972; Harper & Row, 1972)

Johns, Philip, *Within Two Cloaks* (William Kimber, 1979)

Johnson, Brian, *The Secret War* (BBC Publications, 1978; Methuen, N.Y., 1978)

Jones, R.V., *Most Secret War* (Hamish Hamilton, 1978; as *The Wizard War*, Putnam, 1978)

Jowitt, William, *Some Were Spies* (Hodder & Stoughton, 1954; Musson, Toronto, 1954)

Kahn, David, *The Codebreakers* (Weidenfeld & Nicolson, 1966; Macmillan, N.Y., 1967)

Kahn, David, *Hitler's Spies* (Hodder & Stoughton, 1978; Macmillan, N.Y., 1978)

Kersten, Jacob, and McMillan, James, *The Secret of Torgau* (Harrap, 1982)

Kesaris, Paul (ed.), *The Rote Kapelle* (University Publications of America, 1979).

Korganoff, Alexandre, *The Phantom of Scapa Flow* (Ian Allan, 1974)

Kimche, Jon, *Spying for Peace* (Weidenfeld & Nicolson, 1961; Roy, N.Y., 1962)

Knatchbull-Hugessen, Sir Hughe, *Diplomat in Peace and War* (Murray, 1949; Transatlantic Arts Inc., Florida, 1949)

Kramarz, Joachim, *Stauffenberg* (Andre Deutsch, 1967; Macmillan, N.Y., 1967)

Kurz, Hans, *Nachrichtenzentrum Schweiz* (Verlag Huber, 1972)

Landau, Henry, *All's Fair* (Putnam, 1934)

Landau, Henry, *Secrets of the White Lady* (Putnam, 1935)

Langley, J.M., *Fight Another Day* (Collins, 1974)

Laurens, Anne, *The Lindemans Affair* (Wingate, 1971)

Leasor, James, *Green Beach* (Heinemann, 1975; Morrow, 1975)

Leasor, James, *The Unknown Warrior* (Heinemann, 1980; as *Code Name Nimrod*, Houghton Mifflin, 1981)

Leverkühn, Paul, *German Military Intelligence* (Weidenfeld & Nicolson, 1954; Praeger, 1954)

Lewin, Ronald, *Ultra Goes to War* (Hutchinson, 1978; McGraw-Hill, 1979)

Lewin, Ronald, *The American Magic* (Penguin, 1983; Farrar, Straus, 1982)

Lewin, Ronald, *The Other Ultra* (Hutchinson, 1982)

Lovell, Stanley, *Of Spies and Stratagems* (Prentice-Hall, 1963)

McCall, Gibb, *Flight Most Secret* (William Kimber, 1981)

McKee, Alexander, *Black Saturday* (Souvenir Press, 1959; Holt, Rinehart & Winston, 1960)

Maclean, Sir Fitzroy, *Take Nine Spies* (Weidenfeld & Nicolson, 1978; Atheneum, 1978)

Mader, Julius, *Hitler's Spionage Generale* (Verlag de Nation, Berlin, 1971)

Maguire, Eric, *Dieppe: August 19* (Cape, 1963; Clarke, Irwin, Toronto, 1963)

Manvell, Roger, *The Conspirators* (Pan, 1972; Ballantine, 1971)

Marshall-Cornwall, Sir James, *War and Rumours of War* (Secker & Warburg, 1984)

Martin, David C., *Wilderness of Mirrors* (Harper & Row, 1980)

Mason, Herbert Molloy, *To Kill The Devil* (Michael Joseph, 1979; Norton, 1978)

Masterman, J. C., *The Double Cross System in the War of 1939–1945* (Sphere, 1973; Yale, 1972)

Middlebrook, Martin, *The Nuremberg Raid* (Allen Lane, 1973; Morrow, 1974)

Montagu, Ewen, *Beyond Top Secret U* (Peter Davies, 1977; as *Beyond Top Secret Ultra*, Coward-McCann, 1977)

Moorehead, Alan, *The Traitors* (Hamish Hamilton, 1952; Scribner, 1952)

Moravec, Frantisek, *Master of Spies* (Bodley Head, 1975; Doubleday, 1975)

Mosley, Leonard, *The Cat and the Mice* (Arthur Barker, 1978)

Mosley, Leonard, *The Druid* (Eyre Methuen, 1982; Atheneum, 1981)

Moyzisch, Ludwig, *Operation Cicero* (Wingate, 1950; Coward-McCann, 1950)

Mure, David, *Practise to Deceive* (William Kimber, 1977)

Mure, David, *Master of Deception* (William Kimber, 1980)

Newman, Bernard, *Spy* (Gollancz, 1935; Appleton-Century, N.Y., 1935)

Newman, Bernard, *Spycatcher* (Gollancz 1945; Ryerson, Toronto, 1945)

Newman, Bernard, *Epics of Espionage* (Werner Laurie, 1950; Philosophical Library, N.Y., 1951)

Newman, Bernard, *Inquest on Mata Hari* (Hale, 1956; McGraw-Hill, Toronto, 1956)

Newman, Bernard, *The World of Espionage* (Souvenir, 1962; Ryerson, Toronto, 1967)

Newman, Bernard, *Spies in Britain* (Robert Hale, 1964; T. Allen, Toronto, 1964)

Padfield, Peter, *Dönitz: The Last Führer* (Gollancz, 1984; Harper & Row, 1984)

Page, Bruce, and Knightley, Philip, *Philby, The Spy Who Betrayed a Generation* (Andre Deutsch, 1968; as *The Philby Conspiracy*, Doubleday, 1968)

Paine, Lauran, *The Abwehr* (Robert Hale, 1984)

Peis, Gunter, *The Mirror of Deception* (Weidenfeld & Nicolson, 1977)

Perles, Alfred, *Great True Spy Adventures* (Arco, London and New York, 1956)

Perrault, Gilles, *Secrets of D-Day* (Arthur Barker, 1965; Little, Brown, 1965)

Perrault, Gilles, *The Red Orchestra* (Arthur Barker, 1968; Simon & Schuster, 1969)

Peskett, S. John, *Strange Intelligence* (Robert Hale, 1981)

Philby, Kim, *My Silent War* (McGibbon & Kee, 1968; Grove Press, 1968)

Piekalkiewicz, Janusc, *Secret Agents, Spies and Saboteurs* (David & Charles, 1974; Morrow, 1973)

Pincher, Chapman, *Their Trade is Treachery* (Sidgwick & Jackson, 1981; Bantam, 1982)

Pinto, Oreste, *Spycatcher* (Werner Laurie, 1952; Harper & Row, 1952)

Pinto, Oreste, *Friend or Foe* (Werner Laurie, 1953; Putnam, 1953)

Popov, Dusko, *Spy-Counterspy* (Weidenfeld & Nicolson, 1974; Fawcett, 1975)

Porten, Edward von der, *The German Navy in World War II* (Arthur Barker, 1977; Crowell, 1971)

Rado, Alexander, *Codename Dora* (Abelard-Schuman, 1977)

Read, Anthony, and Fisher, David, *Operation Lucy* (Hodder & Stoughton, 1980; Coward-McCann, 1981)

Reiss, Curt, *Total Espionage* (Putnam, 1941)

Reynolds, Quentin, *Dress Rehearsal* (Angus & Robertson, 1943; Random House, 1943)

Robertson, Terence, *Dieppe* (Hutchinson, 1963; McClelland & Stewart, Toronto, 1963)

Roosevelt, Kermit, *The War Report of the OSS* (Walker, 1976)

Roskill, Steven, *The Navy at War* (Collins, 1960; as *White Ensign: The British Navy at War*, US Naval Institute, 1960)

Rothfels, Hans, *The German Opposition to Hitler* (Oswald Wolff, 1961; Regnery, 1962)

Roon, Ger van, *German Resistance to Hitler* (Van Nostrand Reinhold, London and New York, 1971)

Rowan, Richard, *Spy and Counter-Spy* (John Hamilton, 1928; Viking Press, 1928)

Ruland, Bernd, *Die Augen Moskaus* (Schweizer Verlaghaus, 1973)

Ryan, Cornelius, *A Bridge Too Far* (Hamish Hamilton, 1974; Simon & Schuster, 1974)

Sansom, A.W., *I Spied Spies* (Harrap, 1965; Clarke, Irwin, Toronto, 1965)

Schellenberg, Walter, *The Labyrinth* (Andre Deutsch, 1956; Harper & Row, 1956)

Schlabrendorff, Fabian von, *The Secret War Against Hitler* (Hodder & Stoughton, 1966; Copp, Clarke, Toronto, 1966)

Schramm, Wilhelm von, *Conspiracy Among Generals* (Allen & Unwin, 1956; Scribner, 1957)

Schwarz, Urs, *The Eye of the Hurricane* (Westview, 1980)

Shirer, William, *Berlin Diary* (Hamish Hamilton, 1941; Knopf, 1941)

Singer, Kurt, *Spies and Traitors of World War II* (Prentice-Hall, 1945; as *Spies and Traitors*, W. H. Allen, 1953; Singer Books, California, 1953)

Singer, Kurt, *The Men in the Trojan Horse* (Beacon Press, 1953)

Singer, Kurt, *More Spy Stories* (W. H. Allen, 1955; Singer Books, California, 1955)

Singer, Kurt, *Spy Omnibus* (W. H. Allen, 1959; Denison, 1960)

Smith, Bradley, and Agarossi, Elena, *Operation Sunrise* (Andre Deutsch, 1979; Basic Books, 1979)

Snyder, Gerald, *The Royal Oak Disaster* (William Kimber, 1977; Presidio Press, 1976)

Stafford, David, *Britain and European Resistance 1940–1945* (Macmillan, 1980; University of Toronto Press, 1980)

Stevenson, William, *The Bormann Brotherhood* (Arthur Barker, 1973; Harcourt Brace, 1973)

Stevenson, William, *A Man Called Intrepid* (Macmillan, 1976; Harcourt Brace, 1976)

Stevenson, William, *Intrepid's Last Case* (Michael Joseph, 1984; Random House, 1984)

Strong, Kenneth, *Intelligence at the Top* (Cassells, 1968; Doubleday, 1969)

Strong, Kenneth, *Men of Intelligence* (Cassells, 1970; St Martin's Press, 1972)

Sweet-Escott, Bickham, *Baker Street Irregular* (Methuen, 1965)

Thomas, John Oram, *The Giant Killers* (Michael Joseph, 1976; Taplinger, 1976)

Thompson, R. W., *Dieppe at Dawn* (Hutchinson, 1956; as *At Whatever Cost*, McGraw-Hill, Toronto, 1956; White Lion, 1973)

Thomson, Sir Basil, *Queer People* (Hodder & Stoughton, 1922)

Toland, John, *Infamy* (Methuen, 1982; Doubleday, 1982)

Trepper, Leopold, *The Great Game* (Michael Joseph, 1977; McGraw-Hill, 1977)

Trevor-Roper, Hugh, *The Philby Affair: Espionage, Treason and Secret Services* (William Kimber, 1968)

Troy, Thomas, *Donovan and the CIA* (University Publications of America, 1981)

U-47's War Diary (Brassey's Naval Annual, 1948)

Waagenaar, Sam, *The Murder of Mata Hari* (Arthur Barker, 1964; as *Mata Hari: A Biography*, Appleton, 1965)

Weiner, Jan, *The Assassination of Heydrich* (Pyramid, 1966; Grossman, N.Y., 1969)

Wighton, Charles, and Peis, Gunter, *They Spied on England* (Odhams, 1958; as *Hitler's Spies and Saboteurs*, Holt & Co, 1958)

Wheatley, Dennis, *Stranger Than Fiction* (Hutchinson, 1959)

Wheatley, Dennis, *The Deception Planners* (Hutchinson, 1980)

Whitehead, Donald, *The FBI Story* (Muller, 1957; Random House, 1956)

Whitehouse, Arch, *Espionage and Counterespionage* (Doubleday, 1964)

Whitehouse, Arch, *Epics and Legends of the First World War* (Muller, 1964; as *Heroes and Legends of World War I*, Doubleday, 1964)

Whiting, Charles, *The Spymasters* (Saturday Review Press, N.Y., 1975)

Winterbotham, F.W., *Secret and Personal* (William Kimber, 1969)

Winterbotham, F.W., *The Ultra Secret* (Weidenfeld & Nicolson, 1974; Harper & Row, 1974)

Winterbotham, F.W., *The Nazi Connection* (Weidenfeld & Nicolson, 1978; Harper & Row, 1978)

Wohlstetter, Roberta, *Pearl Harbor: Warning and Decision* (Stanford, 1962)

Young, A. P., *The 'X' Documents* (Andre Deutsch, 1974)

Index

True war – now available in Panther Books

Len Deighton		
Fighter	£2.50	☐
Blitzkrieg	£1.95	☐
Tim O'Brien		
If I Die in a Combat Zone	£1.25	☐
Larry Forrester		
Fly for Your Life	£1.50	☐
Edward Young		
One of Our Submarines	£1.95	☐
G S Graber		
The History of the SS	£1.50	☐
William Manchester		
Goodbye, Darkness	£2.95	☐
Peter Shankland and Anthony Hunter		
Dardanelles Patrol	£1.50	☐
Kitty Hart		
Return to Auschwitz	£1.95	☐
Angus Calder		
The People's War	£3.95	☐
Wolf Heckmann		
Rommel's War in Africa	£2.95	☐
Viktor Suvorov		
Inside the Soviet Army	£2.95	☐
John Winton		
The Death of the Scharnhorst	£2.50	☐

To order direct from the publisher just tick the titles you want
and fill in the order form.

True war – now available in Panther Books

Alexander Baron From the City, From the Plough	£1.95	☐
C S Forester Hunting the Bismarck	£1.50	☐
Ka-Tzetnik House of Dolls	£1.95	☐
Olga Lengyel Five Chimneys	£1.95	☐
Dr Miklos Nyiszli Auschwitz	£1.95	☐
Alexander McKee Dresden 1945	£2.50	☐
Bruce Myles Night Witches	£1.95	☐
F Spencer-Chapman The Jungle is Neutral (illustrated)	£1.95	☐
Bryan Perrett Lightning War: A History of Blitzkrieg	£2.50	☐
Leonce Péillard Sink the Tirpitz!	£1.95	☐
Richard Pape Boldness Be My Friend	£2.50	☐
Ian Mackersey Into the Silk	95p	☐
Baron Burkhard von Mullenheim-Rechberg Battleship Bismarck	£2.95	☐
Livia E Bitton Jackson Elli: Coming of Age in the Holocaust	£1.95	☐
Charles Whiting Siegfried: The Nazis' Last Stand	£2.50	☐

To order direct from the publisher just tick the titles you want
and fill in the order form.

True crime – now available in Panther Books

To order direct from the publisher just tick the titles you want
and fill in the order form.

All these books are available at your local bookshop or newsagent, or can be ordered direct from the publisher..

To order direct from the publisher just tick the titles you want and fill in the form below.

Name _____

Address _____

_____

Send to:
Panther Cash Sales
PO Box 11, Falmouth, Cornwall TR10 9EN.

Please enclose remittance to the value of the cover price plus:

UK 45p for the first book, 20p for the second book plus 14p per copy for each additional book ordered to a maximum charge of £1.63.

BFPO and Eire 45p for the first book, 20p for the second book plus 14p per copy for the next 7 books, thereafter 8p per book.

Overseas 75p for the first book and 21p for each additional book.

Panther Books reserve the right to show new retail prices on covers, which may differ from those previously advertised in the text or elsewhere.